TRIUMPH
PRE-UNIT TWINS

Other Titles in the Crowood MotoClassics Series

TRIUMPH
PRE-UNIT TWINS

Matthew Vale

THE CROWOOD PRESS

First published in 2012 by
The Crowood Press Ltd
Ramsbury, Marlborough
Wiltshire SN8 2HR

www.crowood.com

British Library Cataloguing-in-Publication Data
A catalogue record for this book is available from the British Library.

ISBN 978 1 84797 323 8

Designed and typeset by Guy Croton

Printed and bound in Malaysia by Times Offset Sdn Bhd

CONTENTS

PREFACE

When the Triumph Speed Twin was introduced to the British public in the late summer of 1937, few people could have predicted the impact that it would have on the British and world motor cycle market; indeed, the name still has a resonance in the 21st century, with the current Triumph Speed Triple. Edward Turner, the Triumph Engineering Company's general manager, chief designer and minority share holder had a flair for identifying what the market wanted, and in the late 1930s the Speed Twin was that model. It marked the beginning of Triumph's and Turner's three-decade domination of the British motor cycle industry. At a stroke, the Speed Twin rendered the ubiquitous British single obsolete, and for most of the other British manufacturers it marked the start of a long period of decline. All the major industry players struggled to match, and arguably never managed to surpass, the Speed Twin in the decades that followed its introduction.

Turner's Triumph Twin remained in production in one form or another from 1937 to 1988 – more than 50 years – with only the interruption of World War II and a short break between 1983 and 1985 when production moved from Meriden to Devon. This is a record unmatched by any other British manufacturer and of all the world's motor cycle manufacturers, only Harley Davidson can approach this record with its V Twins.

The Triumph Pre-unit Twin range began in 1937 with the Speed Twin, which was supplemented by the sports Tiger 100 in 1939. After the war a new 350cc bike was added to the range, the off road sports Trophy arrived and in 1949 the 650cc Thunderbird was added. Throughout the 1950s the model range concentrated on the 500cc and 650cc bikes and the range became more and more successful, culminating with the introduction of the 650cc T120 Bonneville super sports model in 1959. The Pre-unit twin range was superseded by the more compact Unit Construction models in the late 1950s and early 1960s, but remains one of the most popular ranges of bikes in the world.

This book looks at the Pre-unit range of Triumph Twins, giving a model-by-model description of all the bikes in the range and a technical description of the main elements of the bikes. The history and background of the Triumph factories that made them and their impressive competition successes are detailed. The impressions of riders and owners are also recounted, including the experiences of riders who owned the bikes in the past and owners who still ride them on today's busy roads.

ACKNOWLEDGEMENTS

Many thanks to Ken Moorhouse, Tony Sumner, Bruce Simpson, Peter Horwood, Chris Bunce and Paul Mansfield for information and photographs of the various Triumphs they own or have owned.

Rowena Hoseason and Frank Westworth of RealClassic (www.realclassic.co.uk) once again helped with the provision of various photographs, and through them many thanks also to Kay Fitzgibbons of focusedimage.com.au, who provided some fine pictures of T120 Bonnevilles and Tiger 110s.

Rob Stockdale runs www.tiger100.co.uk and gave me permission to use some of the information he has researched around the specifications of the pre-war Triumph twins.

GB Motorcycles of Withycombe, Station Road, Christian Malford, Wiltshire SN15 4BG (telephone +44(0)1249 720448/+44(0)77111 56919 is a classic bike dealership and was kind enough to provide me with a number of pictures of the 1950 Triumph 3T De-luxe. They can also be found online at www.gbmotorcycles.com

Vrnltd – vrnltd@yahoo.co.uk – is a classic bike dealership located in Cheshire (PO Box 1, Northwich, Cheshire (telephone +44(0)1928 788500/ +44(0)7979852000) which also trades on ebay as vrnltd and gave me permission to use the pictures of the 1949 Triumph 3T.

Thanks also to Rockerbox, (31 The Street, Wrecclesham, Farnham, Surrey (01252 722973)), a traditional bike shop with a strong Triumph bias, for help and advice and access to a very nice Trophy.

Kevin Dean ('Kevin the Bodger') from the RealClassic website also supplied some fine pictures.

Finally, many thanks to my wife Julia and daughter Lizzie, who once again put up with me vanishing off to the study and various bike shows, museums and jumbles while researching and writing this book.

CHAPTER 1

TRIUMPH, TURNER AND THE PRE-UNIT TWINS

Masterminded by the design talent of Edward Turner, Triumph introduced its idea of what a vertical twin-cylinder motor cycle should be with the Speed Twin of 1938. While this was not the first British vertical twin-powered motorbike, it was the right bike at the right time. After a motorcycling 'diet' from the mainstream manufacturers comprising singles of various capacities, unwieldy 'V' Twins and expensive 4-cylinder exotica such as the Matchless Silver Hawk and Ariel Square Four, the British motorcycling public was ready for a new concept in motorcycling. Up to then the four-stroke single, in 350cc or 500cc form, had been the machine of choice for the average

enthusiastic rider, and Turner's Twin looked like a single, weighed the same (or less) than a single, was smoother than a single and had a sparkling performance that was as good as the best sports single but was tractable and easy to ride.

With two cylinders it was considered to be a 'multi' and a cut above the ubiquitous singles. With all these features and an affordable price, it was an immediate success. When they were introduced, the bikes featured separate engines, primary drives and gearboxes. When Triumph (and other manufacturers) introduced power units with engine, primary drive and gearbox encased in a single pair of castings in the late 1950 and

The Speed Twin was produced from 1938. With a rigid frame and girder forks it was a definitive pre-war motor cycle. With its Amaranth Red finish and chrome tank, it was an attractive proposition even before considering the technical appeal of its twin-cylinder engine.

early 1960s, the new models were introduced as 'Unit Construction' and became known as Unit Twins, and the original models became known retrospectively as the 'Pre-unit' range. The Second World War stopped production of the twins, but at the end of the conflict they were rushed back into production to feed ever expanding home and export markets desperate for personal transport. All the other British factories introduced their own take on the vertical twin in the post war market, but the Triumph twin always seemed to be a step ahead in performance and popularity, and it dominated the market all through the 1950s and 1960s. Ultimately, the Triumph Twin was to remain in production until the late 1980s, when all the rivals had fallen by the wayside.

After the introduction of the Twin and its re-introduction after World War II, success in the US market gave Triumph large profits and a great degree of independence through the 1950s, despite being sold to BSA in 1951, and the company entered the 1960s with a wide product range and an excellent reputation. The Pre-unit Twins were eventually succeeded by Unit Construction models in the late 1950s and early 1960s, but the range remains a firm favourite with enthusiasts.

The Triumph Engineering Company

Edward Turner

The fortunes of the Triumph Engineering Company from the 1930s through to the 1970s were inextricably entwined with Edward Turner, a gifted engineer and larger than life personality. After serving in the Merchant Navy during World War I and working as a fitter and turner while gaining his engineering qualifications at night school, Turner had bought a small motor cycle business – Chepstow Motors in Peckham, southeast London, which had an agency for Veloce motor cycles – in the early 1920s.

It was in this shop that he started his long association with the motor cycle industry. His first design was for a single-cylinder, 350cc four-stroke engine with a gear-driven single overhead camshaft. The design was featured in *The Motor Cycle* of 16 April 1925, but never got off the drawing board. But Turner moved on and in early 1927 designed a new 350cc single, which featured a shaft driven overhead face cam. This engine was built and mounted in a Turner-

Edward Turner's first design to make it into production was the complex, sophisticated Ariel Square Four.

The Triumph 6/1 was a 650cc vertical twin designed by Val Page. Primarily a sidecar lugger, it was discontinued by Turner when he took over Triumph.

designed frame with Webb front forks, rigid rear end, saddle fuel tank and Sturmey-Archer hand-change gearbox. The bike was called the Turner Special and was road registered. It featured in the 6 January 1927 issue of *The Motor Cycle* and a second prototype, with much improved styling, was built. Nevertheless, the model never made it into production, since Turner could not find the financial backing needed. So he 'got on his bike' as the saying goes, and went to Birmingham, then the centre of the British motor cycle industry, to lobby the major players in the industry for a job as a designer, using the Turner Special as an example of his skills. Luckily, Turner had also begun thinking about a unique configuration for a multi-cylinder engine, the square four.

Vic Mole, sales manager at Ariel, saw Turner and was intrigued by the square four concept. He arranged for Turner to be interviewed by Ariel's chief designer, Valentine (Val) Page and Jack Sangster, joint managing director. Page and Sangster were impressed with Turner and his concept. In January 1929 Turner was engaged as a development department designer and engineer. At Ariel, Turner developed his ideas for a square four motor, essentially a pair of vertical twins coupled together, into the Ariel Square Four. It became the flagship of the Ariel range and remained in

production into the late 1950s. His future success with vertical twin engines was based on his experience of the four, and the twin's layout was essentially half a square four.

Updates and the Tiger

The Triumph Engineering Company was formed in 1936 when Sangster purchased the motor cycle interests of the Triumph Company, which had decided to concentrate on the motor car market. The deal was for a short-term lease and an option to buy the Triumph motor cycle premises, plant and machinery in Dale Street, Coventry. This site, also referred to as the Priory Street works since it fronted onto Priory Street as well as Dale Street, was a five-storey building incorporating a factory and full supporting facilities, including a canteen and a nurse's surgery. It was where 'The Triumph' (as the workers referred to the company) would be located until the enforced move to Meriden during World War II.

The lease on the premises enabled Sangster to continue production of the Triumph motor cycle range with little or no disruption, and he later consolidated the new firm's position by taking up the option to buy the buildings and the site. Sangster installed Edward Turner, his protégé from Ariel, as the general manager and, importantly, chief designer. Turner was given a 4.9 per cent shareholding in the new company and paid a 5 per cent commission on net profit. His record at Ariel was good, with the innovative Square Four his most famous design, but he also had an uncanny knack for identifying what the buying public wanted. His first job at Triumph was to update the current range. It comprised 250cc, 350cc and 500cc singles, and the 6/1 650cc twin, all designed by Val Page, who had joined the original Triumph company in 1932.

Turner began by modifying the 250cc, 350cc and 500cc sports models, producing the Tiger 70, Tiger 80 and Tiger 90, and improving the appearance of the existing bikes with a light re-style and new paint schemes. The 6/1 twin was dropped from the range. It was not a particularly sporting mount, since its long stroke configuration was not conducive to high power output and the heavy engine was married to substan-

This Triumph 2H or 3H is an example of the singles produced by Triumph in the 1930s, before Turner gained control.

tial cycle parts, making it more suited to sidecar duties. It did not suit the young and sporting image for Triumph that Turner wanted, and this, combined with poor sales, led to Turner dropping it.

While Turner was sorting out the new company's products, Jack Wickes, a qualified draftsman and talented designer, was appointed as Turner's personal assistant. He was responsible for putting many of Turner's ideas and sketches into finished designs – Turner recognised his talent and referred to him as 'his pencil'. Wickes remained at Turner's side throughout the production run of the Pre-unit Twins and had an important role in turning Turner's styling ideas into reality.

The Tiger name chosen for the re-vamped singles demonstrated Turner's flair for catchy names, while the numbers signified the top speed attainable by each model (or at least planted the ideal top speed in the mind of the punter), but probably the most significant feature of the new machines was their styling. The bikes boasted chrome-plated fuel tanks and headlamp shells and an attractive light blue paint scheme on the fuel tank panels and mudguards, giving them slim and sporting lines. And the changes were more than skin deep, with minor tuning including polished flywheels

to cut oil drag and head porting and stronger valve springs to give a boost over the standard models.

A team of three singles, ridden by Ted Thacker on a 250, Allan Jefferies on a 350 and Fred Povey on a 500cc, won gold medals in the 1936 International Six Days Trial (ISDT). After this achievement the new Tiger range won the Auto Cycle Union (ACU) Maudes Trophy in 1937, giving sales and Triumph's prestige a major boost. To win the Trophy, three bikes, a Tiger 70, a Tiger 80 and a Tiger 90 were plucked at random from various dealers' stock by the ACU and delivered to the Donnington Park race circuit. There, Ted Thacker, Allan Jeffries and Freddie Clark, riding the 70, 80 and 90, respectively, and after a day's delay due to inclement weather, performed a three-hour speed test supervised by ACU observers. The following day the bikes were taken to the Brooklands circuit, where maximum speeds of 66.39mph (Tiger 70), 74.68mph (Tiger 80) and 82.31mph (Tiger 90) were recorded. In October 1937, the ACU announced that it had awarded Triumph that year's Maudes Trophy. Nevertheless, while these changes and achievements helped sell the existing range, Turner was working on a new product that would take Triumph to the next level and turn it into a truly world class outfit.

The Introduction of the Speed Twin

The product Turner was working on was designated 5T and named Speed Twin. It was a 500cc vertical twin-cylinder masterpiece. Although he had dropped the 6/1, Turner knew the merits of the twin-cylinder configuration, benefits still worthy today, for the motor cycle and, more importantly, the market was ready for something different. The vast majority of affordable sporting mounts in the mid-1930s were 350cc or 500cc singles, with little to differentiate between the various manufacturers' machines.

The Speed Twin, therefore, really re-defined the British motor cycle industry. It was as light and wieldy as the average 500cc single, but gave better performance owing to the combustion chamber efficiency of a twin, was smoother and had better power characteristics than a single and, probably most importantly, it looked superb. In addition, from a distance it could be mistaken for a twin-port single and so appealed to the notoriously conservative motorcyclist of the day, since it did not look unusual or outlandish; in fact it used most of the Tiger 90's running gear and looked similar as well. The Speed Twin once again displayed Turner's uncanny ability to produce attractive designs that appealed to motorcyclists. The bike backed up its good looks with performance; with its engine producing a claimed 29bhp at 6,000rpm, an honest top speed of over 90mph (149km/h) was readily available, with flexibility and excellent in-gear acceleration.

A contemporary road test in the 21 October 1937 issue of *The Motor Cycle* gave an average top speed over four runs of 93.75mph (150km/h), with a one-way best of 107mph (172km/h), although the magazine did concede that it was a very windy day! The bike's finish was another of Turner's masterpieces. The 3½Imp gal (15 litre) fuel tank was in polished chrome, with Amaranth Red panels lined with gold pinstripes and had black rubber knee grips. The frame, forks, mudguards, tool box, oil tank and remaining running gear were also painted in Amaranth Red, a dark, rich shade that would become a Speed Twin 'trademark'. The large 8in (203mm) chrome-plated headlamp set off the front end, while the centres of the chrome wheel rims were painted in Amaranth Red and, like the tank, lined with a gold pinstripe. The alloy timing cover, gearbox end cover and the large alloy primary

This 350cc Tiger 80 shows how Turner's restyle gave the range a new sporting appeal.

The tank-top instrument panel of the Tiger 80 was suitably sporty.

From the drive side, the slim pre-war Speed Twin can easily be mistaken for a twin-port single.

The pre-war Tiger 100 was a sensation, with the looks and performance to attract sales.

chain case were polished to add to the effect. All in all, the appearance was striking but not flashy and along with the advanced mechanics, made for a very attractive whole.

The Speed Twin not only went well and looked good, but it also sold well. The bike got a very positive reaction from the press of the day, and the public also liked it and bought it. Unlike the 6/1, the Speed Twin gave the public what they wanted, a sophisticated, multi-cylinder bike that was affordable, handled like a single and topped it off with good looks and performance.

The Speed Twin was also introduced to the American market through the Triumph distributor of the time, Reggie Pink. While Pink was not a big player, he managed to import about 100 Triumphs before the war, giving Triumph a toehold in the market, which was reinforced by the efforts of Triumph's Canadian distributors, Sammett and Blair (Eastern side) and Nicholson Brothers (Western side) who were also selling Triumphs to the USA while meeting the demand from Canada. Thanks to the efforts of these organisations, small but significant numbers of Speed Twins and Tiger 100s had made their way into the US, alongside the singles, in the years before World War II.

With the Speed Twin a resounding success, Turner produced a second model to address the sports market. Introduced in late 1938 for the 1939 model year, the Tiger 100 followed the naming convention adopted for the sporting singles. It also followed the styling cues of the sporting Tiger range, with black cycle parts and Shell Blue mudguards and tank panels, neatly differentiating it from the Speed Twin. The fuel tank was slightly larger, with a 4Imp gal capacity, but was similar in shape and profile to the Speed Twin unit. With a lightly tuned engine giving approximately 33bhp, 4bhp or 13 per cent up on the Speed Twin, the performance of the Tiger 100 lived up to its name, with a top speed of just under 100mph (160km/h) being achieved in the Motor Cycling test of 16 November 1938.

In 1939 the Tiger 100 featured in Triumph's bid to win the Maudes trophy again. For this attempt a Speed Twin and a Tiger 100 were selected by the ACU, from dealers in Biggleswade and Sheffield, respectively. The bikes were then run from Coventry up to John O'Groats, then on to Land's End and back to the

Brooklands motor racing circuit at Weybridge. The 1,806-mile (2,906km) route was covered at an average speed of 42mph (68km/h). Then, at Brooklands, with Ivan Wickstead and Dave Whitworth on the Tiger 100 and Freddie Clark and Allan Jefferies on the Speed Twin, both bikes were run for six hours round the track. The Tiger 100 averaged 78.5mph (126.3km/h) and the Speed Twin 75mph (120.7km/h).

The only mechanical problem occurred when the Tiger 100's oil pressure gauge pipe fractured during the Brooklands run, a problem easily fixed by hammering it flat. In November 1939 it was announced that Triumph had been awarded the trophy.

Back in September 1939, a confident Triumph had already been poised to exploit the market for sporting multi-cylinder machines, and things looked bright for the new company. But storm clouds were gathering with the ever-increasing belligerence of Herr Hitler.

This 1939 Tiger 100 shows the model's slim lines and sporting stance.

Wartime Production

Great Britain declared war on Hitler's Germany on 3 September 1939 and this would have unforeseen consequences for Triumph. Production of the Speed Twin and its sporting derivative, the Tiger 100, continued after the declaration of war and through the 'Phoney War' of 1939 and early 1940. However, the introduction of the 350cc 3T and Tiger 85 twins for the 1940 range was stopped and production of the 1940 model year Speed Twin and T100 was very limited, as military needs had to be addressed.

The War Office had bought two Speed Twins for assessment in December 1939 and the whole factory stock, including Speed Twins and Tiger 100s, was impressed at the end of 1939. In total, some 1,400 machines were delivered for military service during the first six weeks of the war. However, in early 1940 the immediate demand for military machines had been met and during the Phoney War the factory was able to manufacture civilian machines for the home and export markets.

At the beginning of World War Two, Triumph had already incorporated a number of improvements into its range and a few 1940 models were produced. This is a brochure shot of a 1940 Speed Twin.

This is the 1940 Tiger 100 – few were produced before production was turned over to the war effort.

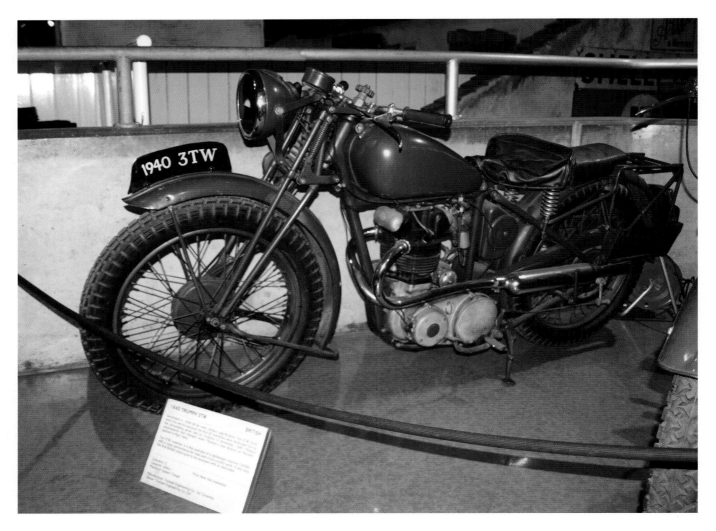

The 3TW was Triumph's first attempt at designing a military motor cycle from scratch.
The first production batch was lost in the blitz of 1940.

A number of 500cc side-valve 5SW machines were also produced during March 1940, to meet a French military order. After the Dunkirk evacuation of May 1940 and the loss of virtually all the British Army's motorised transport, which was left in France by the British Expeditionary Force, the 3SW (350cc side-valve single) and 5SW models were ordered in bulk by the War Office. While these were the main motor cycles being produced, post-Dunkirk some 140 3H 350cc overhead-valve singles were also delivered.

In addition to these bikes, the works produced a range of other military goods, including two-wheeled stretcher carriers, tank track links and numerous aircraft components. In addition to this production effort, development of a specific military machine had been started before the war around a government specification that called for a bike weighing less than 250lb (113kg) and with a capacity greater than 250cc. Triumph's 350cc twin-cylinder 3TW was designed to meet the requirement and prototypes were under test during 1939. Production was sanctioned in late 1940, following a further series of tests. The first batch of 50 production bikes had almost been completed and many were crated up ready for despatch when bombs fell on the Coventry factory during the Luftwaffe raid on the night of 14 November 1940. Virtually the whole batch was destroyed.

The WD 3HW single replaced the 3TW when the factory resumed production in Warwick and Meriden. Based on the pre-war single, it gave sterling service.

While the air raid resulted in the complete destruction of the Dale Street buildings, the 120 night shift workers had plenty of warning to get to the shelters, which proved their worth, since incredibly no one was killed. The only reported injury was to a worker who tripped over in the darkness and damaged his ankle.

Aware of the importance of production to the war effort, Triumph immediately took over an old disused foundry in nearby Warwick and moved in everything that could be salvaged from Dale Street, to resume production in double quick time. Machine tools, undamaged components, raw materials and drawings were among the myriad items moved to the temporary works to get production up

and running. The foundry was already named 'The Cape' so the Triumph staff nicknamed it 'The Cape of Good Hope'. The factory offices were housed in a former chapel close to the foundry. Constructed from corrugated iron, it soon gained the irreverent nickname 'The Tin Tabernacle'. Two or three of the 3TW bikes were salvaged, one being tested by *The Motor Cycle* in its 6 March 1941 issue.

Initially the Warwick factory produced spares for the existing Army machines, but by June 1941 production of complete machines, mainly the 3SW, had commenced. Some of the less damaged parts of the Dale Street works had also been repaired and were contributing to production.

During this time at Warwick, Turner had a row with Sangster over their inability to agree what reward Turner should get from Triumph's use of his patents and in 1942 Sangster summarily dismissed Turner. As a result Turner moved to BSA, leaving the Triumph Company without a leader. However, Bert Hopwood, who had joined Triumph as Turner's Design Assistant in 1936, was in overall change of engineering and so the Company was in good hands. Initially Triumph wanted to move back to the Dale Street location once it had been rebuilt, since a survey showed that most of the vital services were intact and many of the workers lived nearby, but the site was considered to be too vulnerable to further air raids and Coventry Council also had other plans for the city centre. So while production continued at The Cape of Good Hope and in the remains of the Dale Street works, Triumph was planning and designing a new purpose built factory four miles outside Coventry on a green field site just off the main Coventry to Birmingham road, between the villages of Meriden and Allesley. The site was soon named the Meriden Works and Triumph moved there in 1942. Post-war, the Meriden Works became the home of 'The Triumph'. It was where all post-war Triumph Twins were produced until 1983.

Meriden and the Ascent of Triumph

The Meriden factory was all new and equipped with a combination of new machine tools and others salvaged from Dale Street and moved from Warwick. The building work was completed and fitting out began in early 1942, with some areas becoming operational in the spring and the factory being fully operational by the autumn. The plant comprised purpose-built assembly and office areas and was a welcome change from both the old Dale Street works and the temporary Warwick premises. Hopwood described it as "a transition from slum to palace" and the company was able to redesign its production lines and facilities from scratch, resulting in probably the most modern and best laid out factory in the British motor cycle industry. Production concentrated on the 350cc single-cylinder overhead-valve 3HW, since the War Office had decided to concentrate on 350cc overhead-valve and 500cc side-valve singles. Other military work included design and

production of various types of portable generator unit for the RAF, which spawned a self-contained winch unit for naval target towing aircraft.

While Turner was over at BSA, Jack Sangster heard that he was designing a 500cc side-valve twin for the military, and decided that Triumph would design a 'spoiler' twin of its own. The plan was to produce a prototype that was not intended to go into production, but would be shown to the press before the announcement of Turner's BSA design. Hopwood was not impressed with the plan, since it diverted design effort from important wartime production, but he succeeded in producing the 5TW, which was presented to the press at the Grosvenor Hotel in London in February 1943. It predated the BSA machine by some months. The bike was in a lot of ways the forerunner of the TRW, and it certainly was not a lightly re-hashed 3TW as some sources have described it. This was not surprising. Hopwood's low opinion of the 3TW was well known and the new bike was considerably beefed up to enable it to survive the rigours of military use. In addition, it was the first Triumph to be equipped with telescopic front forks.

After this diversion, Meriden settled down and continued to produce 3HWs and the other items for the war effort. It also set about planning for peace. Turner returned to Triumph during 1943, after some 14 months at BSA. The main development work then turned back to the side-valve 500cc twin, since the War Office had come to the conclusion that the configuration offered all that it needed for a military motor bike.

The Meriden plant became a major factor in Triumph's post-war success. Through the good works of Turner, the company had already demonstrated that it could identify the product the market wanted, but this could only lead to success if the product was reliable and the factory could meet the demand for the product. The basic design of the Speed Twin was sound and Meriden enabled Triumph to meet the demand, with production running at up to 1,000 machines per week in the 1960s.

As the war drew to a close, Triumph began looking to the future and civilian life. In March 1945 it released details of its post-war range, which comprised the 3H single, the Speed Twin and Tiger 100, and two new 350cc twins, the 3T and the sporting

Triumph reintroduced the Speed Twin, post-war, now equipped with telescopic forks.

Tiger 85, which had originally been announced in 1939 but suffered a delay before going into production! The 3H was a straightforward civilianised version of the then current WD 3HW, with an all-black finish, polished timing and gearbox covers and a chromed exhaust pipe. In line with Turner's eye for making a model attractive to the masses, it was equipped with an alloy primary chain case to replace the WD model's pressed steel unit; the latter had been introduced to save aluminium.

Demand for the twins meant the 3H was never produced in quantity post-war. Indeed, some sources report that none were actually built for public consumption and the model was quietly dropped from the range when the production of the civilian twins got into its stride. While the 'new' 500cc twins were similar to the pre-war specification, all featured new Triumph-designed telescopic front forks, the Tiger 100 was slightly de-tuned to cope with the 72-octane 'pool' fuel then available, and both 500s came with the Tiger 100's 4Imp gal fuel tank. The 3T also had the new telescopic forks, but had a lighter and slightly smaller frame. With victory in Europe celebrated on 8 May 1945, and in the Far East on 14/15 August (depending on the time zone, with the final signing of surrender by Japan on 2 September), Triumph was ready and able to resume production of its civilian machines.

The Rivals

When Triumph introduced the Speed Twin in 1937, it had no real rivals. Triumph's sporty 500cc twin was unique and effectively leading the market. Its 1939 Tiger 100 helped to consolidate this lead, when the only competition was 500cc singles from the other big firms, including BSA, Ariel, and AJS. The Triumph twin outperformed the singles in virtually all aspects – performance, weight and price.

It was only after World War Two that real competitors appeared on the scene, with the other major manufacturers putting 500cc twins into production. BSA's 500cc A7 twin first saw the light of day and became available to buy in 1946, while Ariel's 500cc twin was announced in 1946, but was not available to buy until 1947. The Royal Enfield 500cc twin and the AMC twins, the AJS Model 20 and Matchless G9 came out in late 1948 and, finally, Norton's Model 7 Dominator 500cc twin was announced in 1948 and became available in

The Model 7 Norton 500cc twin was a Speed Twin rival.

1949. The BSA A7 came in rigid or plunger-sprung frames, as did the Ariel. The AJS and Matchless twins came with a swinging arm frame, as did the Royal Enfield, while the Norton was originally equipped with plunger rear suspension. The Speed Twin and Tiger 100 were equipped with the rigid frame with the option of the sprung hub and never had plunger rear suspension. The Triumph swinging arm frame appeared in 1954.

Like Triumph, the competition also produced larger capacity variants based on the original 500cc engines. BSA came up with a revamped pair of twins, the 500cc A7 and the 650cc A10 in 1949 and in 1954 introduced a modern, all-welded swinging arm frame to house both engines. BSA hit the sports market with a sporting 500cc twin, the A7 Shooting Star, to rival the Tiger 100, and various 650cc Rockets with alloy heads to rival the T110. Ariel trod a slightly

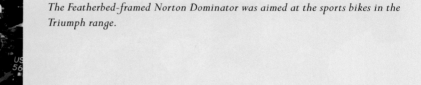

The Featherbed-framed Norton Dominator was aimed at the sports bikes in the Triumph range.

The 1952 500cc AJS Model 20 was a sporting mount aimed at the Tiger 100.

The Rivals *(continued)*

different path, introducing the 650cc Huntmaster in 1954. This used a lightly modified BSA A10 engine and had a new swinging arm frame that was also used for Ariel's 500cc twin, with its Ariel-designed engine. AJS and Matchless introduced new 600cc twins with swinging arm frames in 1956, and introduced a full 650cc twin (for the US market) for 1958. Norton also went down the 600cc route with its 596cc engine for 1955.

Norton introduced a full 650cc motor in late 1960 and this engine grew into the 750cc Atlas unit for 1962. A new swinging arm frame, developed from the plunger version, was introduced in 1953 for the 500cc Model 7 and aimed at the sidecar market, but Norton's main claim to fame was the introduction of the Featherbed frame, with its superlative handling and road holding, for the 1952 Model 88 500cc twin. The 600cc engine was put into the Featherbed and the original

With its softly tuned, all-iron 650cc engine, the BSA A10 Golden Flash was aimed at the 6T Thunderbird.

The sporting BSA A7SS Shooting Star, with its alloy head, was aimed firmly at the Tiger 100.

swinging arm frames in 1956, and the 650 and 750cc engines were also fitted in the Featherbed when they were introduced. A scrambles version of the Norton 600cc twin, the Nomad, designed to compete with the Triumph TR6 in the cross country racing 'Desert Sled' market, was introduced in 1958, using the old pre-Featherbed type frame. The 750cc Norton-engined, Matchless-framed 'Hybrids' were introduced in the mid-1960s after Triumph had gone to unit construction.

Royal Enfield leapfrogged the intermediate engine sizes and introduced a monster 700cc twin to the market in September 1952. Housed in a swinging arm frame, the Meteor 700 was the largest vertical twin at the time and at least matched the performance of the rival 650cc touring twins. Despite their good points, none of the opposing machines were as stylish, or survived as long, as Turner's Twin.

Royal Enfield's 700cc Constellation (this is a 1962 model) was aimed firmly at the T120 Bonneville.

The 350cc 3T was originally scheduled to be produced in 1940, but was eventually introduced in the 1946 model range. This is a 1950 version, with the famous nacelle.

As the US market became more important it began producing its own publicity material. This flyer from 1950 details the models available.

Export or Die

At the end of the war Britain was victorious, but essentially bankrupt. The imperative was to turn wartime production into exportable goods in an attempt to bring in as much foreign currency as possible to pull the country out of its economic hole. Among other controls placed on commerce by the post-war government, supplies of strategic materials such as steel were limited to companies that could produce goods for export.

Triumph was well placed to do this and building on the announcement made in the spring of 1945, the civilian range for the 1946 model year comprised the 350cc 3T, and the 500cc Speed Twin and Tiger 100. The Tiger 85, while listed in the 1946 brochure, never made it into full production as demand for the 500cc twins outstripped supply. From an export perspective, Triumph was particularly well thought of in the USA, through the efforts of Reggie Pink in the pre-war years. However, as the war had progressed, supplies of Triumphs for Pink had dried up and he had had to sign up to sell Harley Davidsons, in an agreement that meant he could no longer sell the British product.

However, Turner had already established contact with a smart Californian attorney, William E. Johnson Jnr, usually known as 'Bill', who had bought an Ariel Square Four in the late 1930s and entered into correspondence with Turner about the machine, which had been designed by Turner during his stint at Ariel. Johnson acquired a small dealership, British and American Motors, in 1938 and spent the next two years selling the Speed Twin, Tiger 100 and various other British makes. The company also sponsored racing with the Tiger 100, following the American idiom of 'Win on Sunday, Sell on Monday' and with Bruce 'Bo-Bo' Pearson won thirty-two out of thirty-six events entered in the 1940 season. In 1940 the company name was changed to Johnson Motors, known in the industry as JoMo, and through Johnson's relationship with Turner, JoMo secured the Southern Californian direct sales rights for Triumph.

Turner visited Johnson at this time, cementing the friendship that had bloomed through the correspondence of the previous years. Despite the lack of supply of Triumphs through the war years, Johnson had kept his company going with contracts for aircraft components from US industry. During 1944, JoMo was signed up by Turner as the official distributor for Triumph and Ariel in the US, and at the end of the war was well placed to satisfy the pent up demand for Triumph Twins. Of course, Triumph now had the production capacity and need to fulfil the demand. JoMo began building a nationwide network of dealers and after a relatively slow start, by the late 1940s JoMo had signed up over 100 dealers and was handling some 1,000 or so of Triumph's annual production of 12,000 bikes.

An aspect of JoMo's marketing strategy was to move away from the traditional rough and tough motor cycle shop image to an image that was attractive to the professional who was interested in motor cycles. To this end, JoMo moved its headquarters to new location in Pasadena, a modern, spacious building that had originally been a car showroom. The building provided the respectable impression JoMo wanted to project to its customers and provided space for the showroom, workshop and offices that were needed.

Soon Triumph and JoMo saw the need for a dedicated East Coast distributor and in late 1950 set up the Triumph Corporation, known as Tri-Cor and wholly owned by the factory. Tri-Cor was based in Baltimore, Maryland, and tasked to look after sales in the whole of the eastern USA. The factory appointed Dennis McCormack, a naturalised American originally from Coventry, to run the organisation.

As well as demand from the USA, Triumph also had a healthy domestic market to address, along with the more traditional Empire markets, with Canada, Australia and New Zealand being particularly good for sales. Nevertheless, the dominant market for the 1950s and into the 1960s was the US and Turner recognised this and planned his product range accordingly.

The Golden Years

At the beginning of the 1950s, Triumph had well established and enthusiastic dealer networks worldwide, plus a fine range of Twins to meet the demand. With the large number of common parts across the range, production costs could be minimised and the Meriden factory could cope with the demands of the transport-hungry public. In the home market, the economic situation was improving. People were

One of the most famous units produced post-war was the alloy-barrelled Tiger 100 unit.

Typical of the Tiger 100 of the 1950s, Ken Moorhouse's machine is a 1956 model.

becoming more affluent and the youth market, with its demands for performance and attractive machines, was taking off, much as the US market had in the early post-war years. In the US it their performance and sporting prowess that was selling Triumphs and demand showed no sign of abating.

The 3T was deleted from the range in 1952, to enable production to be concentrated on the more profitable 500cc and 650cc bikes; with the unique 3T engine no longer being built, the development department could concentrate on the 500cc and 650cc engines. Compared to the 1,000 or so units exported to the US in 1950, JoMo and Tri-Cor sold over 2,700 bikes in 1951 and sales continued to increase in subsequent years. Figures from Triumph, by Ivor Davies, show that exports to the US in 1958 totalled 4,553. The market continued to grow steadily, with sales of 5,725 in 1959 and 6,586 in 1960.

Unfortunately, Triumph's success also led to a number of problems. Jack Sangster wholly owned the company, apart from Turner's minority share, and he saw that if he did not do something then the continued existence of Triumph would be under threat when he died, owing to the level of death duties tax that would become due. So in 1951 Sangster arranged the sale of Triumph to arch rival BSA. The action appeared to have no effect on Triumph, and it continued to be run completely independently of BSA under Turner's iron rule. Triumph's US distribution network also remained under Triumph control and an American town commonly had rival BSA and Triumph dealers, providing good, healthy competition to keep the products of both companies competitive.

As Triumph sales grew steadily throughout the 1950s, the product range increased in breadth, with models like the TR6 being specifically tailored for US

The on/off-road TR6 Trophy was a big success in the USA.

As the 1960s dawned, Triumph paint schemes became brighter, as on this 1960 TR6.

The high point of Pre-unit development was the 650cc twin-carb Bonneville.

tastes. As the decade went on and the North American market became more important, the development of the Pre-unit models was influenced more and more by its demands. In some cases, especially with the TR6 range, models were designed to include East and West coast derivatives.

The development of the whole Triumph range was now heavily influenced by the demands of the US market, resulting in much improved and better focussed models. It was this focus that led to the T120 Bonneville, which marked the peak of development of the Pre-unit range, and, in its 1960 to 1962 guise, was the definitive performance motor cycle across the globe.

The End of the Pre-unit

With the introduction of the Unit Construction 350cc Twenty-one in February 1957, the writing was on the wall for the Pre-unit models. The advantages of Unit Construction were clear. With the engine, primary drive and gearbox carried in a common set of castings, the engine and transmission pack was a lighter and more rigid structure, leading to fewer oil leaks. In addition, there were compelling economic reasons to go with unit construction – the unit bikes were more compact, lighter, used fewer parts and were easier to produce in the factory. These factors also meant that the engine and

The Unit Construction twins appeared in the late 1950s. This is a 500cc 5TA from 1960.

The big Unit twins continued in development all through the 1960s and 1970s. These are 1970 examples of the T120 (left) and TR6 (right).

Model Years

As a company, Triumph manufactured bikes on a yearly cycle that ran from roughly August in the preceding year to about July in the actual year designated for a model, giving rise to the term 'model year'. During a model year, the company would do its best to avoid introducing changes to a model, since it would disrupt production. Each calendar year had a set of specific models associated with it, so, for example, the 1948 model year had the 3T, 5T and Speed Twin models. Since production of a model year's bikes actually started in the autumn of the preceding year, and finished around July of the actual year, a 1948 model year Triumph could have actually been produced as early as August 1947 or as late as July 1948. The date of manufacture can be ascertained from the engine and frame numbers of any Triumph twin and this defines which model year the bike was made in.

While one year's production was being built, the design department would be beavering away during the year to design, test and get ready for production the myriad of changes made to existing models and to introduce new models. The production cycle would run from after the factory closed down for the summer holiday (usually in August) through to the start of the next summer's close down. At this point the production lines would also be closed down and the new parts and models made ready for production when it resumed. After World War 2, the US market became increasingly important for Triumph and much of the production that took place at the start of the new production year would be aimed at the US market so that the completed bikes could be shipped by sea to the USA to reach the East and West Coast distributors in plenty of time to be in the dealers' showrooms in the vital spring selling season, when the majority of new bikes were sold. Once the demands of the US market had been met, then Triumph could concentrate on the home and general export market models. Once that year's production was completed and the factory workers sent off on their holidays, the production line could be changed to take into account the new model features and readied for production to restart at the end of the holidays and the cycle started again.

transmission could be placed in a smaller and lighter frame, and all these factors gave major cost savings. There was less material used to produce each bike and it could be built in less time with less effort. Fewer spares also needed to be produced by the factory and kept in store by dealers and distributors. Finally, the customer considered Unit Construction more modern.

Initially the 350cc Twenty-one placed Triumph in a new market, one uncontested since the demise of the 3T in 1951, but in September 1958 Triumph introduced a new Unit Construction 500cc Speed Twin, based on the Twenty-one.

This bike, the 5TA, replaced the Pre-unit 5T Speed Twin for the 1959 season, and a new sports orientated Unit Construction twin, the T100A, was introduced in 1959 to replace the Pre-unit T100 for the 1960 season. This only left the Pre-unit 650cc twins in production, the Thunderbird, TR6 Trophy and T120 Bonneville, and these were replaced for the 1963 season with the 650cc 'B' series unit twins. The final Pre-unit bikes built were a final batch of 500cc side-valve TRWs against a military order that were completed during 1964.

CHAPTER 2

MODEL DEVELOPMENT

Triumph's range of Pre-unit twins was produced from 1937 through to 1962. In this time there was a wide range of variations on the theme, with capacities ranging from 350cc through 500cc and up to 650cc. The bikes were produced as road orientated tourers and sports mounts, a pure road racer, versatile on/off road mounts and, in the TRW, as a standard military motor cycle for NATO forces.

The table below provides the model years during which the main production models of the Pre-unit range were produced.

The range began with the Speed Twin in 1938, joined by the Tiger 100 in 1939. The war precluded manufacture of a civilian range, with the exception of some 1940 model year bikes, and after the destruction of the Dale Street works and the move to Meriden, production concentrated on singles for the war effort.

Meriden set the scene for post-war production – it was modern, new and exciting. The post-war range was going to be an all-twin line up, although the 1946 range brochure included a WD-based 350cc single. The new post-war twin range also included the 350cc 3T twin, as well as the Speed Twin and Tiger 100, and the factory also listed the Tiger 85, a sporting 350cc twin based on the 3T, although none were produced.

The sprung hub was introduced in 1947 as an optional bolt-on rear suspension system to compete with rivals' plunger systems. The famous TR5 Trophy off-road sports model hit the streets in 1949, along with the 650cc 6T Thunderbird, introduced to meet the US demand for more performance. The 650cc TR6 Trophy took over from the TR5 in 1956. Production demands saw the 3T deleted from the range in 1951, and the first single down tube swinging-arm frame was introduced for 1954. It was followed by the duplex down tube frame in 1960.

Model	Capacity	Type	Introduced	Final Year
Speed Twin 5T	500cc	Road – Tourer	1938	1958
Tiger 100	500cc	Road – Sports	1939	1959
3T De-luxe	350cc	Road – Tourer	1946	1951
Grand Prix	500cc	Road Racer	1946	1950
TRW	500cc	Military	1948	1964
Thunderbird 6T	650cc	Road – Tourer	1949	1962
Tiger 110	650cc	Road – Sports	1953	1961
Trophy TR5	500cc	On/Off Road	1949	1959
Trophy TR6	650cc	On/Off Road	1956	1962
Bonneville T120	650cc	Road – Sports	1959	1962

By then the 500cc Pre-unit bikes had been superseded by the 'C' series Unit Construction twins, the 5T Speed Twin by the 5TA in 1959, and the Tiger 100 by the T100A in 1960. The Tiger 110 sports model appeared in 1953, but was deleted from the range in 1961, with its place as the top-of-the-range sportster taken by the T120 Bonneville, introduced in 1959. The 650cc Pre-unit twins, the 6T Thunderbird, the TR6 Trophy and the T120 Bonneville soldiered on until the end of the 1962 model year, when the 'B' series 650cc unit twins superseded them.

The main anomaly in the production life of the Pre-unit range was the TRW. This was produced in batches throughout the life of the Pre-unit range, with the final batch completed during 1964, well after production of the rest of the Pre-unit twins range had finished.

It is worth noting here that all of the Pre-unit Triumphs produced between 1949 and 1964, apart from the Trophy models, employed 1in diameter handlebars. Triumph's move to industry standard 7/8in diameter bars only came about when the Pre-unit models were replaced by the Unit Construction ranges.

Speed Twin

5T Speed Twin 500cc 1938–1959

The Speed Twin, designated by Triumph as the 5T, was revealed to the public in the autumn of 1937 for the 1938 model year. It is fair to say that it was very well received by press and public alike. It was described as 'one of the outstanding machines at the Earls Court Motor Cycle Show' in *The Motor Cycle* test of 21 October 1937, and the test goes on to say that the bike 'amply fulfilled the high claims made by its makers; its all round performance was surprising'; and despite the polite 'trade speak' used by the magazines of the time to avoid upsetting their advertisers, the use of 'surprising' did not mean the test bike's performance was surprisingly low!

With the new engine placed in what was essentially a Tiger 90 frame and running gear, and with the twin's engine narrow enough to avoid changing the

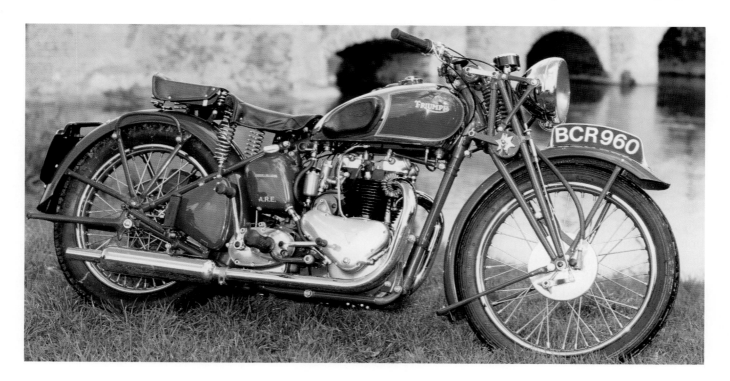

The pre-war Speed Twin was an inspired design that appealed to the contemporary motorcyclist.
Good looks combined with class leading performance was a winning combination.

The 1938 Speed Twin had a cast iron barrel and head. This example has the early six stud barrel fixing.

Tiger 90 chain line, Triumph and Turner knew they would have to tread a careful path between showing that the Speed Twin was something really new, and avoiding alienating the traditionally conservative motor cycle buying public.

Turner managed this difficult exercise masterfully. The Speed Twin capitalised on the successful Tiger 90 lines, which was not surprising given that most of the running gear came from that model, and it looked lithe, slim and sporting. The bike's technical innovation, its twin-cylinder powerplant, was so narrow that it could be mistaken for a twin-port single so offered little to offend the traditionalist. The major innovation that marked the bike out from the singles was its finish. The deep plum red Amaranth Red was used for the frame, girder forks, tool box, oil tank, fuel tank panels and centres of the wheel rims. The rich red was nicely set off by chromed wheel rims, exhaust pipes, silencers and 8in headlamp, and the crowning feature was the chromed fuel tank with its lined painted panels. The speedometer was mounted

at the top of the forks and there was a diamond shaped black Bakelite instrument panel in the fuel tank, carrying the ammeter, oil pressure gauge, light switch and inspection light. A single sprung saddle and optional pillion pad finished off the look. The whole effect was very pleasing. It was classy and sporting, and appealed to most potential buyers of the time. Turner's eye for what the market wanted was certainly accurate with the Speed Twin.

So what did the Speed Twin offer the 1930s' motor cyclist? It weighed about the same as the Tiger 90 and 5H singles at a claimed 365lb (165kg) and shared those bikes' dimensions, with a 54in (1370 mm) wheelbase, 84in (2130mm) overall length and low saddle height of 27½in (705mm).

With its engine giving a claimed 28.5bhp at 6,000rpm, it produced only a fraction more power than the 28.29bhp claimed for the Tiger 90, but substantially more than the standard-tune 5H at 23bhp. The twins' power characteristics were also different to those of the singles; with double the number of

This pre-war Speed Twin shows the slim lines and stylish finish that helped make the model a sales success.

power pulses, one per revolution, the Speed Twin had a much smoother performance than either single. The Speed Twin's engine was found to be flexible and useable, but possessed a performance that was just as good, if not better than that of the Tiger 90. Road tests gave great emphasis to its ability to trickle along comfortably in heavy traffic and still perform incredibly well on the open road, with little need to fiddle with the ignition timing to take hills and get more than acceptable acceleration, in contrast to the more sporting singles of the day. So considering the Speed Twin as a touring mount, a stance justified by the introduction of the Tiger 100 in 1939, it offered all the docility and easy controllability of the current range's 5H single, combined

with the performance of the Tiger 90. The test carried out by *The Motor Cycle* in 1937 actually managed to get a best timed run over the quarter mile of 107mph. Over four runs in both directions, the average speed was still a respectable 93.75mph (150km/h).

Manufacture continued into the 1940 model year with a small number of Speed Twins and Tiger 100s built before the factory turned over production to the war effort. The 1940 Speed Twins gained the Tiger 100's frame, with its increased trail, 4Imp gal fuel tank and modified girder forks with check springs. The Bakelite instrument panel was found to be prone to cracking and so was replaced with a steel unit with a crinkle black finish.

Speed Twin Technical Comparison Table

	1937 Speed Twin	1948 Speed Twin (sprung hub)	1958 Speed Twin (swinging arm)
Engine			
Bore × stroke (mm)	63 × 80	63 × 80	63 × 80
Capacity (cc)	497	497	497
Compression ratio	7:1	6.5:1	7:1
Power (bhp @ rpm)	28.5 @ 6,000	28.5 @ 6,000	29 @ 6,000
Carburettor			
Type	Amal 276	Amal 276	Amal Monobloc 376/25
Specification	15/16 bore, 140 main jet,	15/16 bore, 140 main jet,	15/16in bore
	right hand side float bowl	left hand side float bowl	
Number	1	1	1
Transmission			
Engine sprocket (teeth)	22	22	22 (sidecar 19)
Clutch sprocket (teeth)	43	43	43
Gearbox sprocket (teeth)	18	18	18
Rear sprocket (teeth)	46	46	46
Gear ratios (solo)			
Fourth	5.0:1	5.0:1	5.0:1
Third	6.0:1	6.0:1	5.95:1
Second	8.65:1	8.65:1	8.45:1
First	12.7:1	12.7:1	12.2:1
Gear ratios (sidecar)			
Fourth	5.8:1	5.8:1	5.8:1
Third	6.95:1	6.95:1	6.9:1
Second	10.03:1	10:1	9.8:1
First	14.73:1	14.7:1	14.15:1
Wheels and tyres			
Tyres, front	20 × 3.00	19 × 3.25	19 × 3.25
Tyres, rear	19 × 3.50	19 × 3.50	19 × 3.50
Front brake (diameter/width)	7 × 1⅛in (177 × 28.5mm)	7 × 1⅛in (177 × 28.5mm)	7in (177mm)
Rear brake (diameter/width)	7 × 1⅛in (177 × 28.5mm)	8in (200mm) sprung hub	7 × 1⅛in (177 × 28.5mm)
Dimensions			
Seat height	27¾in (704mm)	29½in (750mm)	30½in (775mm)
Wheelbase	54in (1370mm)	55in (1400mm)	55½in (1410mm)
Length	84in (2130mm)	84in (2130mm)	85½in (2170mm)
Ground clearance	5in (127mm)	4in (100mm)	5in (127mm)
Weight	365lb (166kg)	374lb (170kg)	390lb (177kg)
Fuel capacity	3½Imp gal (15ltr)	4Imp gal (18.2ltr)	4Imp gal (18.2ltr)
Oil capacity	6 pints (3.4ltr)	6 pints (3.4ltr)	5 pints (2.8ltr)

World War Two Generator Units for the RAF

Triumph's wartime output was not limited to motor cycles. Among other products, the company also designed and manufactured a self-contained mobile generator for the Royal Air Force, which used a twin-cylinder 500cc engine derived from the Speed Twin unit. Produced from 1943 and still in production in 1946, the unit was designed to be light enough to be carried by two men, but powerful enough to drive a 6kW generator.

Triumph used its twin-cylinder expertise as a basis, and came up with an engine unit that, while similar to that of the Speed Twin, was substantially different in execution. It featured an alloy cylinder barrel and head for lightness and better heat dissipation, and unique aluminium alloy bottom end castings and crankshaft. Remaining a 360-degree parallel twin and using the Speed Twin bore and stroke dimensions and valve gear layout, the unit was lightweight and durable. The alloy crankcases were completely different from those of the Speed Twin. They were extended on the drive side to allow the casing of the 6kW British Thompson Houston (BT-H) generator to be bolted directly to them. The cylinder head had a high-expansion iron casting forming a 'skull' to carry the valve seats and spark plug hole, and the light alloy head was cast around this. The inlet

and exhaust valves had identical diameters, rather than using larger inlets as on the Speed Twin, since the generator did not need to rev as high as the roadster unit. Like the head, the alloy block was cast around iron liners, which had integral bosses to receive the cylinder head studs, thus avoiding having vulnerable alloy threads that could be easily stripped. The alloy block was square in profile to fit the metal cooling shrouds and had eight fins. A distinguishing feature was the two cast-in lugs on each side of the barrel between fins 1 and 2, and 7 and 8, which were drilled and threaded for the cooling shroud to be bolted on. The crankshaft ran on a white metal bush main bearing on the timing side and incorporated a dog for a cranking handle to start the motor. The guide for the starter handle was 'U' shaped and bolted onto each side of the fan housing to form a lifting handle. The sparks were provided by magneto, driven by gears from the timing side exhaust camshaft pinion.

A very noticeable change from the Speed Twin unit was that the exhaust and inlet camshafts were swapped over, with the exhaust camshaft at the 'rear' of the engine and used to drive the magneto. This meant that the cylinder head was reversed and the exhaust ports were over the magneto, which was in the same position as the pre-war Speed Twin's magdyno. The inlet camshaft pinion drove a governor mechanism that was connected to the carburettor and ensured the engine maintained a steady 4,000rpm in use. This enabled it to drive the generator while it gave its peak output of 200 amps at 30 volts, the sort of power needed to kick a Bristol Hercules or Rolls-Royce Merlin engine into life after it had been left out on a frosty airfield! The engine gave 15bhp at the governed 4,000 rpm and was cooled by a fan, connected on the timing side, with the air directed over the cylinder and head using steel shrouding, which left the fronts of the rocker boxes and the round tappet covers exposed for servicing.

The fan could supply 400cu ft (11.3m^3) of air per minute to the engine, and secondary ducting fed air to the generator. The generator was mounted on the drive side and was driven by a coupling from the drive side of the motor, which incorporated a ratchet mechanism so that a kick starter could be fixed in place for alternative means of starting. Hopwood recounts how the coupling gave the only problem with the unit. Initially Turner specified a rubber shock absorber coupling that could not absorb the high cyclic speed variations

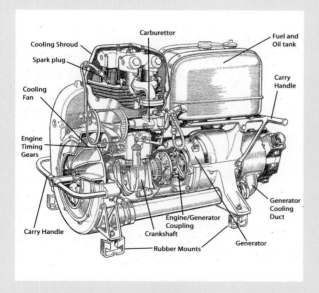

The RAF generator was a compact and portable unit.

(continued overleaf)

World War Two Generator Units for the RAF *(continued)*

imposed on it and kept breaking. This was eventually superseded by a cam-type shock absorber, which solved the problem. The lubrication system followed the Speed Twin practice, but the plunger oil pump was uprated and had just under double the throughput of the Speed Twin unit and a Vokes fabric oil filter was incorporated on the return side. The complete engine/generator unit had a mounting at each corner that could have a vibration-resistant bush fixed to it if the generator was mounted in an aircraft or on a trolley.

The combined fuel and oil tank, which carried 3Imp gal (13.6ltr) of petrol and 5 pints (2.8ltr) of oil, was mounted on top of the generator on its own tubular subframe, which also served as a lifting handle.

The unit came in two variants. The ground unit, usually mounted on a trolley with two motor cycle-type wheels to provide mobility, was used to provide power for charging aircraft batteries, starting engines and powering lighting and other electrical systems while an aircraft was on the ground. The Airborne Auxiliary Power Plant (AAPP – shortened to 'A Squared P Squared' by factory personnel) was, among other uses, carried onboard pathfinder Avro Lancasters to power the extra electronic equipment fitted to these aircraft.

Another development was for an engine capable of driving a larger capacity generator, resulting in a 700cc 4-cylinder unit. This was loosely based on a pair of 350cc 3T units coupled together to form a 4-cylinder 700cc unit, and, like the 500cc AAPP unit, used light alloy barrels with cast-in iron liners and a new pair of alloy cylinder heads mounted on a set of unique crankcases with a specially designed crankshaft. The light alloy heads were very similar in design to the 3T's iron head, with the rocker spindles incorporated in the head casting and access to the valve adjusters through a single large alloy cover front and rear. As on the twin-cylinder generator unit, the fining was squared off to allow for cooling cowls, and the spark plugs were mounted vertically in the centre of the combustion chamber. Examples of these alloy heads and barrels were later used on the works 3T-based trials bikes used by the works team with some success in the late 1940s. Production of the generator units finished shortly after the end of the war, but the alloy cylinder heads and barrels from the AAPP were used on the GP and Trophy production bikes, while the 350cc works 3T trials bikes of 1947 used the alloy barrels and heads from the 700cc 4-cylinder unit.

Without the engine's cooling cowl, the magneto can be seen behind the exhaust pipes, showing how the head was reversed on the generator unit.

The GP and early Triumph Trophy used generator engine-type castings for their head and barrel. Note the cast-in lugs on the barrel for the cooling cowling.

Post-war Speed Twins

Post-war the Speed Twin was placed in the middle of the range, ahead of the 350cc 3T but behind the Tiger 100, and this was reflected in its pricing. The 1946 model was very similar to the 1940 model but with two major changes, the introduction of Triumph's new telescopic front fork and the switch from the Magdyno to a separate magneto and dynamo.

While the magneto remained in position behind the barrels, the 40-watt Lucas dynamo was placed on the front of the engine and the front engine plates had holes in them to accommodate it. Gears from the inlet and exhaust pinions drove both the magneto and dynamo. The headlamp shrank to 7in (177mm) diameter and was chromed for 1946, but painted Amaranth Red from 1947. It was carried on a pair of slim, curved ears on the front fork shrouds. The shrouds ran from the top yoke down to the fork seal holders to cover and weatherproof the join between the slider and the stanchions. The overall colour for the frame, forks, mudguards, panels, oil tank and tool box

remained Amaranth Red and the fuel tank was still chromed, with Amaranth Red panels and gold lining.

The bike carried on in this form until 1949, when the tank top instrument panel was deleted and the famous Triumph nacelle was introduced. This pressed steel item was a stylised streamlined cover for the top of the front forks, carrying the headlamp unit forwards on a chromed adaptor piece, the speedometer, ammeter, light switch and kill switch on the top half. The two-part lower half extended downwards to form the fork stanchion covers. The handlebars and cables sprouted out of the top half, with rubber gaiters used to make a neat interface with the lower section. The upper and lower halves were held together with small screws and the join was covered on each side by a neat, chromed trim piece. The first 800 or so units fitted across the range had alloy lower halves due to a shortage of steel pressings. Since the nacelle did not have room for the oil pressure gauge, a pop-out indicator in the pressure release valve body, mounted on the side of the timing cover, replaced it. The petrol tank now carried a neat, chromed, three-bar parcel grid, fixed

The early post-war Speed Twin had telescopic forks and from 1949 featured the trademark Triumph nacelle.

Early, unrestored Speed Twins still turn up. This immediate post-war example was pictured at the Netley Marsh autojumble in 2010.

in place with four screws. The dynamo was uprated to a 60-Watt unit. A Triumph designed and patented air filter built under licence by Vokes was fitted behind the oil tank and connected to the carburettor by a rubber tube. The air filter element was oil wetted and reusable after cleaning.

From 1950 the petrol tank lost its chrome plating, taking an all over Amaranth Red finish, while the tank badge gained a backing strip of four chromed bands. The new, stronger gearbox, introduced to cope with the 650 Thunderbird's power, was fitted and Triumph also offered its twin seat as an option. The Speed Twin continued largely unchanged to 1952, when the nacelle was modified with a larger diameter for a more commanding look, a small separate pilot or parking light was positioned below the headlamp and the frame had a new seat tube with an 'eye' through the middle to give a clear run for air from the new 'D'-shaped Vokes air filter to the carburettor. Due to the Korean War, the 1952 model had a reduced amount of chrome plating, as well as painted handlebars and wheel rims, while the kick start lever, clutch operating arm, and finned clamps for the exhaust pipes were all cadmium plated.

By the early 1950s the Speed Twin was playing second fiddle to the more sports orientated bikes in the range and the larger, touring Thunderbird, but for the 1953 model year it was used to introduce a major feature that would set the trend for motor cycle electrical systems for the next 20 years. This was the AC alternator electrical system, using a Lucas RM12 alternator that replaced the dynamo and magneto. The Speed Twin was used to prove the system to the customer before introducing it onto the other bikes in the range. The new alternator rotor was fitted to the drive-side end of the crank, with the stator mounted in the outer chain case. The modification resulted in a new primary chain case with a pressed steel, round inspection cover, a new clutch incorporating a rubber vane shock absorber and deletion of the dynamo drive and fixing points. This also meant new crankcases, timing cover and front engine plates.

A two-plate Westinghouse rectifier was fitted under the seat and two switches for ignition and lights were fitted into the nacelle. They were used to switch coils in and out to give rudimentary charging control.

All Triumph twins had alloy primary chain cases. This example shows the stylish bulge over the crankshaft shock absorber.

An ignition distributor and points unit was fitted to the old magneto position and the ignition coil was mounted above it to provide the sparks. The ignition switch had an 'emergency' position for full alternator output in case the battery was flat. The two switches for ignition and lights were replaced by a single, combined unit in 1954, and a new more efficient circular, four-plate rectifier replaced the square Westinghouse unit.

The 1955 Speed Twin inherited the new swinging arm frame introduced the previous year and was the first Triumph fitted with the new Amal Monobloc carburettor, along with a stronger crankshaft with larger big end journals. The 1956 model received the 6T type crankcases and the pilot light was repositioned within the headlamp. A small chromed grill covered the horn, just below the headlamp. By now the replacement for the Pre-unit Speed Twin was being designed and changes to the bike were minimal. A new mouth-organ tank badge was fitted for 1957, along with a 7in diameter full width front hub, while the Slickshift gearbox was introduced in 1958. This was virtually the end of the line for the

model, although about 40 units were built in the 1959 model year. Even in its final incarnation, the bike was finished overall in Amaranth Red.

The Speed Twin was superseded by the Unit Construction 5TA, also named Speed Twin, for the 1959 model year. It featured Triumph's new fully enclosed rear end styling, known as the 'Bathtub'. The 5TA was derived from the 350cc 3TA Twentyone. It was another 500cc twin that used the T100 engine layout but had the engine, primary drive and gearbox in a single set of crankcases. The new Speed Twin and the Twenty-one were regarded as having a modern and compact layout and were termed the 'Unit Twins'. The term 'Pre-unit' was therefore retrospectively applied to the 5T and its derivatives.

The 5TA also moved from the original Speed Twin's 63 × 80mm bore and stroke to 69 × 65.5mm, giving an under-square motor that could tolerate higher revs due to reduced piston speeds. In a nod to its genes, the 5TA was also finished in Amaranth Red, but this was changed for a brighter shade of red for 1960.

This 1958 Speed Twin is close to the end of the Pre-unit line. Note the swinging arm frame, full width front hub, and distributor and coil ignition in the old magneto position behind the barrels.

The 1958 Speed Twin came with coil ignition and an AC alternator in the redesigned primary chain case.

This 1958 Speed Twin shows that the Triumph tank rack was still fitted in 1958, along with the nacelle.

The Speed Twin was a slim bike, and was little wider than a 500cc single.

Tiger 100 500cc 1938–1959

As a sports version of the Speed Twin, the Tiger 100 boasted a tune-up, a revised frame, a new paint job and a catchy, sporty name. The Tiger 100 name used the format already made popular by the revamped singles range and conveyed the expected top speed of the model.

The Tiger 100 finish was dominated by the new wider, chromed 4Imp gal fuel tank, with top and side panels pained in Silver Sheen – a light Silver blue shade – and hand lined in darker blue. The tank carried 'Triumph' script chromed badges, and the tank-top instrument panel, as fitted to the Speed Twin, was retained. Black rubber knee grips were fitted behind the tank badges and gave the rider positive grip. The mudguards and wheel rim centres were also finished in Silver Sheen, again with blue lining. The rest of the motor cycle was finished in black, including the frame, forks, 8-pint (4.55-litre) oil tank and tool box. With the tuned engine came the eight stub barrel fixing to deal with the increased power and the exhaust system featured the distinctive 'cocktail shaker' silencers, with detachable end caps.

The Tiger 100 was introduced in 1939 as a sports version of the Speed Twin.

The 1939 Tiger 100 was finished with a black frame, and silver sheen mudguards and tank panels. This differentiated it from the Speed Twin.

Tiger 100 Technical Comparison Table

	1939 Tiger 100	1948 Tiger 100 (Sprung hub)	1959 Tiger 100 (Swinging arm)
Engine			
Bore × stroke (mm)	63 × 80	63 × 80	63 × 80
Capacity (cc)	497	497	497
Compression ratio	7.75:1	7.8:1	8:1
Power (bhp @ rpm)	33 to 34 @ 7,000 (open megaphone)	33.34 @ 7,000	32 @ 6,300
Carburettor			
Type	Amal Type 76	Amal Type 76	Amal Monobloc 376/35
Specification	1in	1in	1in
Number	1	1	1
Transmission			
Engine sprocket (teeth)	22	22	22 (solo); 19 (sidecar)
Clutch sprocket (teeth)	43	43	43
Gearbox sprocket (teeth)	18	18	18
Rear sprocket (teeth)	46	46	46
Gear ratios (solo)			
Fourth	5.0:1	5.0:1	5.0:1
Third	6.0:1	6.0:1	5.95:1
Second	8.65:1	8.65:1	8.45:1
First	12.70:1	12.70:1	12.2:1
Gear ratios (sidecar)			
Fourth	5.8:1	5.8:1	5.80:1
Third	6.95:1	6.95:1	6.90:1
Second	10.03:1	10.0:1	9.80:1
First	14.73:1	14.7:1	14.15:1
Wheels and tyres			
Tyres, front	20 × 3.00	19 × 3.25	(Note: US models with QD
Tyres, rear	19 × 3.50	19 × 3.50	wheel had WM3 × 18 rim)
Front brake (diameter/width)	7 × 1⅛in (177 × 28.5mm)	7in (177mm)	8in (203mm)
Rear brake (diameter/width)	7 × 1⅛in (177 × 28.5mm)	8in (203mm) (sprung hub)	7in (177mm)
Dimensions			
Seat height	27¾in (705cm)	29½in (750mm)	30½in (775mm)
Wheelbase	54in (1370mm)	55in (1400mm)	55½in (1410mm)
Length	84in (2130mm)	84in (2130mm)	85½in (2170mm)
Width	28⅛in (723mm)	28⅛in (723mm)	28⅛in (723mm)
Ground clearance	5in (127mm)	6in (152mm)	5in (127mm)
Weight	362lb (164kg)	375lb (170kg)	385lb (175kg)
Fuel capacity	4Imp gal (18.2ltr)	4Imp gal (18.2ltr)	4Imp gal (18.2ltr)
Oil capacity	8 pints (4.55ltr)	8 pints (4.55ltr)	5 pints (2.8ltr)

Girder forks carried an 8in diameter chromed head-lamp as on the Speed Twin. A black Terry's sprung single saddle was fitted and a mudguard-mounted pillion pad and footrests were offered as an option. On its introduction the Tiger 100 was fitted with Triumph's unique 'Rev-o-lator' speedometer, with three printed bands on the dial giving engine revolutions in second, third and top gears — another Turner idea that gave the rider an indication of the engine revolutions without the cost and complication of a separate tachometer. With their end caps removed, the cocktail shaker silencers were transformed into racing-style megaphones to provide a power boost.

Each Tiger 100 was produced with a Test Card, signed by the Chief tester, which certified the output of the engine as measured on Triumph's Heenan and Frode brake tester. This practice was dropped in 1947 after the first year of Tiger 100 production following World War II.

Performance-wise, the Tiger 100 demonstrated a small increase over the Speed Twin's figures. A contemporary road test in the 16 November 1938 issue of *Motor Cycling* gave a best timed top speed over the flying ¼ mile of 97.83mph (157km/h), with a mean of runs in both directions giving 95.74mph (154km/h). Probably the most significant performance measurement was the speed attained at the end of a standing start ¼ mile; the Tiger 100 managing more than 80mph (129km/h) in 15⅕ second, while the Speed Twins managed 74mph (119km/h). The Tiger 100 saw a number of modifications for the 1940 model year, including full-skirted pistons, a new oil pressure release valve and slightly higher gearing, up one tooth on the engine sprocket. The girder forks received a lighter main spring and two external check springs were also fitted. The Bakelite instrument panel was replaced with a pressed steel version following a few breakages. Tiger 100 production ceased in November 1939 along with that of the Speed Twin, although some Tiger 100s were produced in early 1940.

Tiger 100 production started again for 1946 and the changes made to the Speed Twin were also reflected in the Tiger 100 — telescopic forks, separate magneto and dynamo, and 7in diameter headlamp.

The cocktail shaker silencers were no longer fitted, Speed Twin-type units being used. The finish remained as per the pre-war bike, with the new tele-

On its introduction, the 1939 Tiger 100 shared much of its running gear with the Speed Twin. However, the frame geometry was modified to give better high speed handling.

This 1939 Tiger 100 is equipped with the rare bronze head.

The 'cocktail shaker' silencers on the pre-war Speed Twins had detachable ends which, when removed, converted them into racing megaphones. This is a 1940 model — note the check springs on the side of the girder forks.

scopic fork shrouds and sliders in black, and the head-lamp shell also in black rather than chrome. Performance was similar to the pre-war version's. The model had the option of the sprung hub (offered in 1947); otherwise it carried on largely unchanged until the 1949 model year, when the separate head-lamp and instrument panel were replaced by the nacelle, in line with the Speed Twin. The Speed Twin's 6-pint oil tank was also adopted for 1949, allowing accommodation for the new Vokes oiled-element air filter. The gearbox-driven speedometer drive was also standardized. A newly styled fuel tank, with all-painted finish and the four-bar chromed strip between the knee grip and the front of the tank, with a chrome Triumph script badge, replaced the chromed unit. The new tank also had the trademark Triumph tank rack mounted on top.

The close-finned alloy barrel was introduced in 1951, giving a very different look to the motor, and this change in appearance was complemented by the introduction of the Triumph 'Twinseat' dual seat, to replace the Terry's single saddle. It helped make the

In 1951 the Tiger 100 gained a close-finned alloy barrel and head. The engine was both distinctive and attractive.

Tiger 100 look more modern, although the lack of rear suspension other than the optional sprung hub was starting to tell. For 1952 there was a new nacelle, with a pre-focused headlamp unit. The pilot light was now mounted under the headlamp, in a small chromed fixing. This external pilot light was deleted for 1956, when the pilot light was repositioned in the headlamp. The Tiger 100 gained the new swinging arm frame in 1954, and this brought the bike fully up to date, giving it a new lease of life.

Along with the new frame came the beefed-up crankshaft, which, although it was still a three-piece bolt up unit, benefited from larger big end journals. A new 8in front brake with cooling air scoop was fitted to the 'pie crust' single-sided front hub with its wavy spoke flange, and this improved braking performance. The 1955 US models got the 3Imp gal (13.7 litre) TR5-style tank, and the pie crust front hub was replaced with a non-wavy spoke flange to address issues with the previous version cracking.

Development of the Tiger 100 seemed to slow down from now on, with only minor changes, previously seen on the 650cc models, being introduced. In 1956 included new con rods were used, with big end shells, and a chrome trim strip on the centre seam of the fuel tank was installed.

The 1957 models got the mouth organ-style tank badges and, with the introduction of the optional Delta alloy head in 1957, a small number of the TR5R model were produced. For the 1959 model year a Delta-head equipped US market-only model, the TR5AD (D for Daytona specification), was produced, but only 111 were built. Along with the Delta head, the TR5R and TR5AD featured twin carburettors, E3134 cams with 11/8in (28.5mm) diameter followers, 9.0:1 compression ratio pistons, white colour-coded racing valve springs, a Lucas K2FR racing magneto and, finally, a tachometer drive in the timing case, with tachometer mounted on the top yoke.

In line with the rest of the range, the Tiger 100 took the Slickshift gearbox in 1958 and in its last year of production, 1959, it got the one-piece forged crankshaft as used on the Bonneville. The Pre-unit Tiger 100 was replaced by the Unit Construction T100A for the 1960 model year.

The Tiger 100 gained the swinging arm frame in 1954, a year before the Speed Twin.
It brought Triumph's sports 500 right up to date.

The swinging arm Tiger 100 retained the dynamo and magneto
electrics until production ceased at the end of the 1959 model year.

Many Tiger 100s are still in use today. This late example was pictured
at the Ardingley show in 2009.

T100 Grand Prix 500cc 1946–1950

While there were only about 175 Grand Prix machines produced, they kept the Triumph name in the competition limelight in the early post-war years. Evolved from the Freddie Clark-developed Tiger 100 on which Ernie Lyons won the Manx Grand Prix in 1946, the production version was unveiled for the 1948 sales season. It used the generator engine all-alloy top end, with its parallel input and exhaust ports and high compression pistons, giving an 8.3:1 (with

options of 8.8:1 and 12.5:1 for running on alcohol-based fuel) compression ratio. The bottom end benefited from racing camshafts and a manual advance/retard BT-H racing magneto. Twin 1in bore Amal Type 76 carburettors and a megaphone exhaust system helped the bike produce a claimed 40bhp. Each engine was hand built and tested, and housed in a fairly standard Tiger 100 frame with a 20in (508mm) front wheel and a 19in (482.6mm) rear.

Both wheels were built with lightweight Dunlop alloy rims. Standard Triumph telescopic forks were fitted at the front and a sprung hub gave a couple of inches of undamped suspension at the rear, although this was often discarded by racers to save weight.

Additional lugs were brazed on the rear lower chain stays to provide fixing points for rear-set footrests and a reversed gearlever and new brake pedal were used. No kick start lever or mechanism was fitted and the hole in the gearbox outer cover was filled with a rubber bung. The oil tank was based on the pre-war unit with a capacity of 8 pints and an external Vokes oil filter was plumbed into the scavenge side of the system. A notable point was that the rev counter was driven from a gearbox fitted on the inside front of the timing chest, replacing the dynamo and using the existing drive.

The bikes had black frames and oil tanks, and alloy mudguards. The fuel tank was not chromed, but was finished overall in silver sheen with blue lining. The rider perched on a sprung saddle and a 'bum pad' was fitted to the rear mudguard to allow the rider to adopt a racing crouch. The twin performed well on the 80-octane 'pool' petrol available in the post-war years, since the smaller cylinders could be run at higher compression ratios than the dedicated racing overhead camshaft singles from AJS and Norton that formed most of the opposition in the late 1940s. However, improvements to the pure racing single engines, the availability of higher-octane fuel and the massive enhancement in handling that the introduction of the Featherbed frame gave to the Norton singles, spelt the death knell for the essentially roadster-derived Triumph and production ceased at the end of the 1950 racing season. The racers' needs were then catered for by the Triumph Race Kit, which was designed to provide the parts a Tiger 100 owner needed to modify a standard bike to GP specification.

The GP had an all alloy engine produced using the cylinder barrel and head castings originally produced for the World War Two RAF generator units. The barrel castings retained the lugs for the cooling shrouds used on the generators.

The Grand Prix was closely based on the Tiger 100. This example is in the National Motorcycle Museum, Birmingham.

The GP in the Sammy Miller Museum clearly shows the parallel exhaust ports and cooling shroud lugs. This bike bears the signature of Ernie Lyons.

T100C 1953

The T100C (C for Competition) was introduced to the US and UK markets as a separate model in 1953. It was aimed at the road racing enthusiast and produced in small numbers; various sources indicate that a maximum of 260 were built by Meriden. The specification of the T100C was closely based on the Race Kit seen in previous years. The bike came will full road equipment, including the lights, steel mudguards and nacelle of the 1953 T100, with the main difference to the cycle parts being a 1Imp gal (4.44 litre) capacity oil tank.

The engine was tuned more or less to the race kit specification and sported twin carburettors, high compression pistons and E3134 high performance camshafts. Aimed at the clubman and amateur racer, the bike was well received by the public, but not really competitive for road racing in the European market, so was only marketed in the UK. The US market always favoured tuned models for its more off road and oval orientated sport and while the 'C' was offered by the factory only for 1953, it was replaced by the factory tuned and produced T100/R, T100/RR and T100/RS from 1955.

MAGNIFICENT   SPORTING

The
TIGER 100 c

The T100C was supplied by the factory during 1953, fully built up as a racing bike for the clubman.

The T100C came with twin carburettors on parallel inlet tracts.

T100/R, RR, RS – US Flat Track Racer 1955–1959

After production of the Grand Prix finished in 1950, Meriden continued to produce the Race Kit and also produced the T100C for 1953. While the twins were no longer competitive on the European road race scene, they were still very competitive in the US off road orientated sports market and the demand for competition models in the US continued.

To meet this demand Meriden produced a number of small batches of racers for the US Class C dirt track race series. These bikes were designated T100/R for 1955 and 1956, and T100/RR for 1957 to 1959. Small batches of the bikes were built at Meriden to a Tri-Cor specification that ensured they met the AMA race regulations and all were exported to the USA. They were based on the TR5, using its rigid frame and fuel tank, with alloy head and barrel, and the Race Kit. They were also equipped with a special low level exhaust system, with both 1½in (38mm) diameter exhaust pipes running down the timing side of the bike and fitted with a pair of 4in (101.6mm) reverse cone racing. The engine was tuned and had a twin carburettor head (part number E3663), Amal GP carburettors with remote float bowl, E3134 cams with racing tappets, racing valve springs and large inlet valves. The bikes had no front brake, which meant a special 'cotton reel' front hub, no front mudguard and were fitted with a light alloy rear mudguard, single sprung saddle and 'bum pad' on the slim rear mudguard. The nacelle was not fitted and the top yoke was left bare, but the fork legs were protected with rubber fork bellows. The bike also had a fold-up right footrest, bronze valve guides and a BT-H magneto. No lights, generator or battery were fitted. The bikes were sold to privateers on the US racing circuit and used by various US distributor-sponsored riders. The T100/RR superseded the T100/R in 1957, but was broadly similar. The main difference was the use of a unique fuel tank with rear-mounted taps and a large-capacity cylindrical oil tank mounted under the seat.

In addition to the dirt track R and RR types, in 1957 Triumph also produced a T100/RS model, developed for use at US road racing events, such as Daytona and Laconia. The bike had the standard single down tube swinging arm frame and its engine specification was the same as for the T100/RR. Like the RR, there was no nacelle or rubber bellows to protect the fork legs, but the bike did have a front mudguard and the standard 8in front brake with alloy back plate and air scoop. The exhaust system comprised separate small diameter down pipes and a pair of 4in open megaphones. The bike featured the standard UK market fuel and oil tanks, and twin seat. The rear mudguard had a special brace with brackets for competition number plates, while rear set footrests and dropped handle bars were also fitted. Both models drew heavily based on the tuning practiced on the T100 and benefited from Triumph's experience in producing the Race Kit for the UK market.

The US market T100RR was aimed at dirt track/flat track racing.

The T100RR had its exhaust system routed on the right hand side to give clearance for racing on the US oval tracks, with their left hand corners.

The T100RS was a US-market road racer, hence the use of the swinging arm frame.

The T100RS was a rare model, Meriden-built to the order of the US importers.

The T100 Race Kit

From 1951 Triumph dropped its Grand Prix model, but supplied a Racing Kit for the new alloy head and barrel-equipped Tiger 100 introduced that year. The kit provided everything needed to convert a standard Tiger 100 into a reasonably competitive racing machine and was supplied to owners only on receipt of engine and frame numbers. This was a cunning ploy by Triumph with the kit there were few warranty issues – if a bike went 'bang', then the factory could not be held responsible.

The kit contained:

- Pistons and rings, with a choice of compression ratios of 8.25:1 for use with low octane fuel, 9.5:1 for use with 50/50 petrol/benzene mix, or 12:1 for use with alcohol
- A pair of racing lift camshafts
- Racing valve springs
- Two Amal Type 6 Carburettors with dual manifold and remote float chamber, throttle cables and petrol pipes
- Smiths 8,000rpm chronometric tachometer with cable and drive gearbox, which bolted onto the inside of the timing chest where the dynamo resided on the road model
- A replacement 1Imp gal (4.55ltr) oil tank
- Two small-diameter exhaust pipes with megaphones
- One folding footrest (to clear the kick starter)
- Racing-type 'W' bend handlebar
- Regulation oval number plate
- Shortened rear brake rod
- Folding kick-starter pedal
- Complete gasket set

In addition, a close ratio gearbox and lightweight alloy mudguards were available from the factory.

Racing Kit items were listed in a separate section in the 1951 parts manual and Triumph also produced a specific brochure entitled Tuning the Triumph Tiger 100. In the brochure Triumph acknowledged that the resulting bike would not be the best in the field but:

> Whilst it is not claimed that the Tiger 100 in racing form can compete successfully against the Factory Specials made in the tool rooms of certain Companies for the T.T. and other European races, it is a fact that properly prepared and competitively ridden, it will hold its own against any road racing motor cycle which can be purchased by the public.

The brochure goes on to describe the content of the Racing Kit and had a couple of pages to explain to prospective racers how they should approach their racing career:

Fitted into a custom-made box, the Race Kit gave the customer everything needed to convert a Tiger 100 into a club racer.

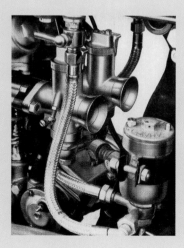

The T100 Race Kit included a new cylinder head and twin carbs.

The T100 Race Kit (continued)

Start in a small way and progress from local club events, grass tracks, etc, to small road circuits, and then by stages to the bigger ones. Learn your limitations, ride in all weathers and watch the Experts – study their methods and ask their advice.

All good stuff, but possibly a little patronising! In addition it gave detailed instructions on how to fit the various components, divided up into Eight stages in Machine Preparation:

- Cleaning the motorcycle
- Removal of engine from frame – step-by-step instruction on getting the engine onto the bench
- Dismantling of engine
- Reassembly of engine – including valve and ignition timing

- Preparation of motorcycle – removal of road equipment and fitting the rear-set footrests
- Replacing engine in frame – with details on setting up the twin carburettors
- Checking and testing
- Fitting close ratio gears to gearbox

The instructions also emphasised the importance of fitting the kit after the bike had been run in on the road and suggested that the owner should cover about 1,000 miles before fitting the Race Kit components. It also praised the sprung hub as being the 'ideal rear suspension unit for racing, being completely rigid laterally and not prone to wear.' No mention of its weight though!

The Racing Kit-equipped engine produced a claimed 42bhp at 7,000rpm, a significant increase over the standard

The twin carbs had a separate float bowl.

The exhaust system used megaphones rather than silencers.

bike's 32bhp at 6,500. As Triumph acknowledged, this was not enough power to be competitive in top class racing, but it gave a good clubman's mount and was successful at club level.

Motor Cycling tested a Racing Kit-equipped swinging arm T100 in 1955, with the test printed in the 21 July issue. With 9.5:1 pistons fitted the bike started easily, even with racing spark plugs, but had an uneven tick over and there was a lot of noise from the valve gear. However, it was found to have vivid acceleration and ran up to a top speed of 116mph (189km/h) at 7,500 rpm, compared with the 100mph being 'within reach when conditions were slightly favourable' from the standard single carburettor T100. Acceleration was compromised by the close ratio gearbox, but the steering and road holding came in for special praise, being described as 'top notch' and 'spot on', despite the

centre stand grounding relatively easily. *Motor Cycling* raced the bike at the 'Silverstone Saturday' race in April 1955 and in the Clubman's race in the Isle of Man, but the article did not say where the bike came. All in all the results of the test implied that the T100 with the Racing Kit was not only an impressive clubman's race bike, but also made an excellent high performance road bike.

The final year of Race Kit availability was 1953; it was still listed in 1954 but none were produced. By then the T100 was equipped with the racing camshafts and the 1953-only T100C had the cams and twin carburettors as standard. For 1954 the twin carburettor head was offered on the T100 as an optional extra, and from then on to the last year of Pre-unit T100 production in 1959, the listings stated that racing conversion parts were available. These included the optional twin carb 'Delta' head of 1957.

The kit included a tachometer drive that replaced the dynamo and used its redundant drive.

The rev counter replaced the speedo in the nacelle.

WD 3TW – 1940

The 3TW was Triumph's first wartime twin-cylinder bike designed for the military. Despite the fact that its gearbox was cast in unit with the crankcases, it is included in this book because of its relationship to the Speed Twin and the 3T Deluxe, and its influence on the later TRW.

It was a victim of the German blitz on Coventry and most of the first production batch was destroyed when bombs hit the Coventry factory in 1940. The 3TW was designed in response to a War Office specification for a four-stroke machine weighing less than 250lb (113.5kg) and with performance equivalent to that of a 500cc side-valve machine. The initial prototype was a 350cc vertical twin with a layout similar to that of the Speed Twin, but displaying a number of features that were based on the aborted 1940 350cc 3T and Tiger 85 twin, that would reappear on the post-war 3T DeLuxe.

The 3TW crankshaft was based on that used for the 3T and comprised two overhung cranks that were spigotted together. They were located and clamped in position on the central flywheel by two nuts and bolts. The one-piece steel connecting rods had white metal applied directly to the face of the big end eyes to provide the big end bearings and at the other end of the connecting rods, the small ends were steel backed lead-bronze bushes. The engine had two gear-driven camshafts front and rear, operating pushrods that lived in tunnels fore and aft of the barrel and produced a

claimed 17bhp at 5,400 rpm. The head incorporated cast-in rocker boxes and rectangular covers for each pair of inlet and exhaust valves. Each cover was held in place by a single central stud. The primary drive had a duplex chain with a slipper tensioner and, probably as a result of Triumph acquiring New Imperial, the three-speed gearbox was in unit with the crankcases, a practice New Imperial employed on its motor cycle engines. In line with Ministry requirements, a large circular air cleaner was incorporated into the timing side of the oil tank and linked to the carburettor by a rubber hose. Girder front forks provided the only suspension, since the rear end was rigid. A 21in (533.4mm) front wheel with 3.00 section tyre, and a 19in (482.6mm) rear wheel with 3.25 section tyre were fitted.

The 3TW also featured a BT-H magneto with automatic advance for ignition, and a small alternator carried in the timing case to give 6-volt direct lighting – a first for a British bike. The frame boasted a mixture of welded and brazed lug construction with a bolt-on rear section. It used the fuel tank as a stressed member to brace the 'swan necked' steering head, the inside of the tank incorporating a 'U'-shaped steel section in a feature later seen on the Tiger Cub and Twenty-one frames. The first prototype was tested during 1939 and fared reasonably well over the prescribed 10,000 miles (16,000km), although the gearbox failed after some 1,600 miles (2,575km) and the direct lighting was not considered to be adequate until 30mph (48km/h) was reached. The first prototype's

The 3TW was in production when the Coventry factory was bombed and most of the bikes were destroyed. This is one of the few survivors.

weight was claimed to be 230lb (104kg) in a test carried out by *The Motor Cycle* during 1941.

The results of the Ministry assessment were fed back to Triumph and a second prototype was produced and supplied to the War Department in early 1940. As wartime shortages and strategic considerations regarding materials started to take effect, the second prototype lost many of the aluminium components, gaining a cast iron head and barrels, but the overall weight only rose to about 260lb (118kg) and did not affect performance. More problems occurred with the gearbox and aluminium replaced the electron casing, which cracked during the test.

A third prototype was also constructed, incorporating a higher riding position and wider footrests, while the engine was given heavier flywheels and a new camshaft, and the alternator was moved into the primary chain case. This was found to be satisfactory by the Ministry and an order was given for production. The first batch of 50 machines had been completed and was being prepared for despatch when the factory was bombed on the night of 14 November 1940. The majority of the bikes were destroyed, although three were retrieved from the wreckage. Despite these improvements and a favourable road test of one of the surviving machines in the 6 March 1941 issue of *The Motor Cycle*, Bert Hopwood had his doubts about the very lightweight construction of the bike and whether it would be 'squaddie' proof. In his memoirs, Hopwood recalls:

> I still feel that, as far as the 50 specials were concerned, Hitler did our War Office a favour. I am sure, and so was Clarke [Freddie Clarke, one of Triumph's testers], that these would proved troublesome in all respects and most certainly were not suitable for the rigours of warfare usage.

After the Coventry blitz, all thoughts of 3TW production had to be put aside as Triumph retrieved what it could from the rubble of the Dale Street works and moved to its temporary facilities in Warwick. At the Warwick facility Triumph had the tooling for the 350cc 3HW single and concentrated on producing it to meet Ministry needs; production of the 3TW was never resumed.

A single example of the 3TW exists. It was displayed in the National Motor Museum, Beaulieu, at the time of writing.

The last surviving 3TW is in the National Motor Museum at Beaulieu. The model had a Unit Construction engine and gearbox, alternator electrics and a cast iron top end.

The 3TW's small three-speed gearbox nestles behind the engine. The engine design was closely based on the 3T unit.

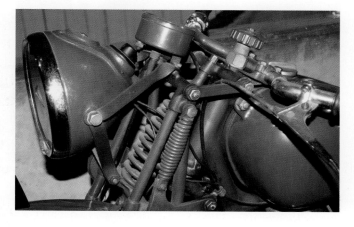

On the 3TW the fuel tank was used as a stressed member to triangulate the steering head, a feature also seen on the Terrier/Tiger Cub range and the first Unit 350cc and 500cc bikes of the late 1950s.

WD 5TW – 1942

During 1941 and 1942, while the factory was operating from Warwick, and after Turner had moved to BSA, a prototype 500cc side valve military motorbike was developed. Some sources say it was designed for comparison to the 3TW, but others, Bert Hopwood included, state that it was produced as a 'spoiler' to steal BSA's thunder. The War Department boffins had been looking at a single model to replace the assorted 350cc and 500cc side valve and overhead valve singles the forces were using. It decided that a side valve 500cc machine would meet their diverse needs. Sangster had also heard that Turner was working on a military 500cc side valve machine at BSA and Hopwood

The spoiler – the 500cc 5TW side valve twin designed by Hopwood to be shown before a similar Turner-designed model from BSA could be demonstrated during the war. The bike was later developed to become the successful TRW. This example is in the London Motorcycle Museum.

was tasked to make a rival that would be announced to the press before the BSA machine. The new bike was known as the 5TW and designed by Bert Hopwood. The prototype was presented to the press in February 1943, ahead of the BSA offering. To save time and development effort, and to overcome the fragility of the 3TW, the bike used Speed Twin-type running gear and a standard, separate four-speed gearbox and telescopic front forks – the first Triumph model to fit them. The engine had a chain rather than gears to drive the front-mounted single camshaft and rear-mounted magneto.

As a spoiler the bike was successful but was never intended to go into production; the war meant that production at Meriden concentrated on the singles. However, the 5TW underwent extensive development under the auspices of a new Ministry of Supply specification for a Universal Military Motor Cycle issued just after the war. In extensively developed form it eventually went into production post war as the TRW.

The London Motor Cycle Museum has a prototype 5TW engine and is in the process of restoring the prototype machine.

3TU 'New Imperial' – 1945

Conceived by Edward Turner as a middleweight utility bike (hence the 'U'), this 350cc twin was intended to be badged as a 'New Imperial' – a brand that had gone bankrupt and ceased production by the beginning of the war and had been bought by Jack Sangster in 1939. The bike was only produced in prototype form during the war years, however, and never made it into production.

It bore little relation to any of the other Triumph twins of the time, but it did incorporate a number of features that would appear on other BSA/Triumph products in subsequent years. Aimed at the commuter market, the 3TU featured many innovations to make it cheap to produce and buy, easy to run and to keep clean, reflecting Turner's increasingly mature views on what the motorcycling public wanted, and predating the scooter boom of the 1950s. The frame was a bolt-up rigid affair with the fuel tank acting as a stressed member in common with the WD 3TW and was later seen in the Tiger Cub and Twenty-one.

The 3TU's engine was a unique 350cc ohv unit. It had coil ignition with a distributor on the top of the timing case and a dynamo behind the barrels.

Designed to be a utility mount and to be badged as a New Imperial, the 3TU was innovative, but did not make it into production. The only example is in the National Motorcycle Museum.

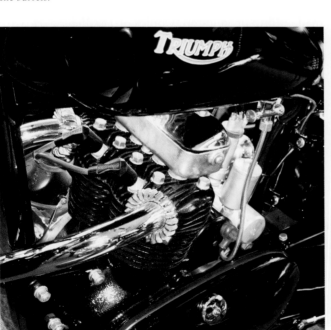

Widely spaced exhaust ports could not prevent the 3TU from having cooling problems and the design was quietly dropped when the success of the larger twins meant there was no production capacity for it.

The Sunbeam S7 inspired much of the thinking behind the 3TU design.

Large, heavily valanced mudguards front and rear provided excellent weather protection, and the design also allowed for the easy fitting of leg shields. The rear mudguard fully enclosed the top half of the wheel, and in its styling it is possible to see the thinking that developed into the 'Bathtub' rear enclosure as seen on Triumphs in the 1950s. The modern-looking telescopic front forks were, unfortunately, undamped. The wheels were 15in (381mm) solid discs, with no spokes and carried large-section (5in; 127mm) tyres to assist with ride comfort, reflecting the same section but larger-diameter balloon tyres fitted to BSA's 1947 Sunbeam S7. Decent sized (for the time) 7in (178mm) diameter brakes were fitted, reflecting those fitted to the Speed Twin.

Electrics were 6 volt, and sparks were provided by coil ignition. The engine was a pushrod-operated, overhead valve twin-cylinder unit, with a single camshaft at the rear. There was a train of gears on the timing side to provide drive, firstly to the forward-facing mushroom-type contact breaker points and sparks distributor, then the camshaft and plunger oil pump, and finally the dynamo, which was placed behind the engine unit above the gearbox. The cast iron crankshaft was a three-part bolt-up unit and the connecting rods were steel pressings (as used on the later Triumph Twenty-one) with split big end eyes and white metal big end bearings. The pushrods ran up behind the engine to aid cooling and the cast iron cylinder head had cast-in towers to carry the rocker spindles and a simple alloy rocker cover perched on top. The spark plugs were placed at the front, inside of the head between the forward-facing splayed exhaust ports and the 'siamesed' exhaust system had an unusually styled silencer on the timing side. Bore and stroke were 57 × 68.6mm, giving a capacity of 350cc. A 1in (25.4mm) Amal carburettor fed the engine from the rear of the cylinder head. In common with other Triumph units, the engine was a dry sump type, with the oil tank on the timing side of the bike, while the cylinder block and the top of the crankcases were cast in iron as one unit, a practice also used on the Triumph Tigress/BSA Sunbeam 250cc scooter of 1958, although the scooter engine was all light alloy.

The gearbox was in a separate casting to the engine. A three-speed unit, it was based on that used in the wartime 3TW twin that never made it into service. The conventional chain driven primary drive was enclosed in a pressed steel case with a central single bolt fixing and a rubber band around its circumference to help keep the oil in. There was provision for a fully enclosed rear chain.

Testing threw up some problems, mainly overheating, and with the Meriden factory going flat out to meet demand for the Speed Twin, 3T and Tiger 100, along with the decision not to revive the New Imperial name, the project was dropped. A prototype remains and is displayed in the UK's National Motorcycle Museum.

3T De-luxe 350cc 1946 – 1951

The 350cc Triumph 3T De-luxe has been described as the Triumph that time forgot. Destined to be eclipsed by the Speed Twin and Tiger 100, it was planned to be in the 1940 model range along with its sporting companion, the Tiger 85. It was initially publicised in *The Motor Cycle* of 8 September 1939, with a front cover proclaiming a 'New 350cc British Twin'.

But with the outbreak of war Triumph made a rapid assessment of what was needed, and neither model made it into production. Copies of *The Motor Cycle* with the introductory article were quickly pulled from the printers and the article was replaced with copy detailing riding in the black out and laying up a machine for the duration. There was a 5½-year delay before the new 350cc models were actually introduced to a bike-starved public in the post-war range announced on 1 March 1945. The 3T De-luxe was produced alongside the 500cc bikes and described by *Motor Cycling* magazine as a bike that: ' …fulfils almost every requirement of the tourist and, in addition, it supplies a performance worthy of a sports specification'.

An interesting point was that none of the other large British manufacturers made 350cc vertical twins at the time, with only the Douglas flat twin offering the 3T any multi-cylinder competition.

While the 3T De-luxe differed significantly from the 500cc bikes in detail, it retained Turner's Triumph look and was well received by the press. It was similar in layout to the Speed Twin and just as handsome, sporting a 31/8Imp gal (14.2 litre) petrol tank finished in chrome with black panels around its tank badges and with the instrument panel set into its top.

Tiger 85 and 3T De-luxe Technical Comparison Table

	1947 3T De-luxe	1947 Tiger 85	1951 3T De-luxe (Sprung hub)
Engine			
Bore × stroke (mm)	55 × 73.4	55 × 73.4	55 × 73.4
Capacity (cc)	349	349	349
Compression ratio	7:1	8:1	6.3:1
Power (bhp @ rpm)	17 @ 6,000	23 @ 7,000	19 @ 6,500
Carburettor			
Type	Amal 275	Amal 275	Amal 275
Specification	120 main, 5/4 slide, 107 needle	120 main, 5/4 slide, 107 needle	120 main, 5/4 slide, 107 needle
Number	1	1	1
Transmission			
Engine sprocket (teeth)	19	19	19
Clutch sprocket (teeth)	43	43	43
Gearbox sprocket (teeth)	18	18	18
Rear sprocket (teeth)	46	46	46
Gear ratios (solo)			
Fourth	5.8:1	5.8:1	5.8:1
Third	6.95:1	6.95:1	6.95:1
Second	10.0:1	10.0:1	10.0:1
First	14.7:1	14.7:1	14.7:1
Wheels and tyres			
Tyres, front	19 × 3.25	19 × 3.25	
Tyres, rear	19 × 3.25	19 × 3.25	
Front brake (diameter/width)	7in (177mm)	7in (177mm)	7in (177mm)
Rear brake (diameter/width)	7in (177mm)	7in (177mm)	8in (203mm)
Dimensions			
Seat height	28¼in (720mm)	28¼in (720mm)	28¼in (720mm)
Wheelbase	53⅛in (1350mm)	53⅛in (1350mm)	53⅛in (1350mm)
Length	82¼in (2090mm)	82¼in (2090mm)	82¼in (2090mm)
Ground clearance	6in (152mm)	6in (152mm)	6in (152mm)
Weight	335lb (147kg)	335lb (147kg)	335lb (147kg)
Fuel capacity	3⅛Imp gal (14.2ltr)	3⅛Imp gal (14.2ltr)	3½Imp gal (16ltr)
Oil capacity	6 pints (3.4ltr)	6 pints (3.4ltr)	6 pints (3.4ltr)

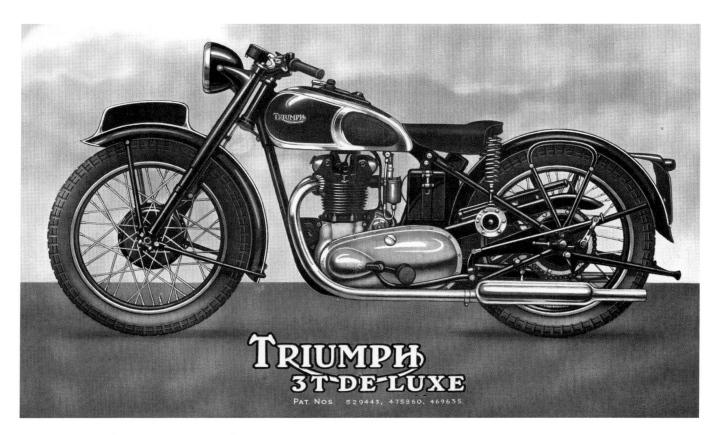

The 3T was supposed to be launched in 1939 for the 1940 season, but the war intervened, and it was properly introduced in 1946.

The black painted panels on the tank were lined with Ivory pin stripes. The rest of the frame and the oil tank and toolbox were black enamel and the chromed wheel rims had a black centre stripe, again lined in Ivory, as was the central stripe on the black mudguards.

The 3T De-luxe's long stroke engine, with its clamped together crank and all-iron top end with integral rocker boxes, shared few components with the Speed Twin and the frame, while similar in layout to that of the 500cc twins, was smaller and lighter; although a derivative was used on the TR5 Trophy models. The exhaust system was unique to the model, and the exhaust pipe entered the silencers at the bottom of the silencer, rather than centrally as on the 500s.

The riding position was criticised as cramped and being more suitable for a smaller rider. With a wheelbase just 1¾in (44.5mm) less than that of the Speed Twin and a 1in (25mm) lower seat height, 3T De-luxe was slightly smaller than the former and a significant 29lb (13kg) lighter. It had a rigid frame and was equipped with the new Triumph telescopic forks, but with a softly tuned engine giving 17bhp, its performance did not compare well with the Speed Twin, with contemporary road tests just scraping a top speed of 70mph (112km/h). However, the bike was considered to be pleasant to ride and made a good tourer; it was probably better than the 350cc singles it was competing against.

With the factory's resources devoted mainly to the larger twins, the 3T De-luxe did not see any significant development during its relatively short production run. For the 1947 model year the sprung hub was offered as an option, and the cylinder head lost its through-bolt mountings. The bike was largely unchanged for 1948, and then gained the stylish nacelle and lost the tank instrument panel, to be

Produced until 1950, the 3T was a pleasant machine but always in the shadow of the Speed Twin and Tiger 100. This is a later model, as identified by its nacelle.

Some 3Ts were exported to the US. High bars were de rigueur in the US and this is an early pre-nacelle model.

replaced by the Triumph tank top parcel grid, in 1949. A new 3½Imp gal (16 litre) fuel tank with an all-black painted finish replaced the chrome plated version for 1950 and incorporated the new 'four bar' chromed tank badge. The bike carried on virtually unchanged into 1951, the final that year the model was listed. By then, the compression ratio had been dropped, but the claimed power output had increased – marketing was probably beginning to intrude on truth.

The 350cc market was significant in the UK pre-war, and continued to be so in the early post-war years, since a 350cc bike could fulfil most riders' requirements, giving a reasonable performance with good economy. However, with the Speed Twin and Tiger 100, Triumph had raised the game and most other manufacturers were also offering 500cc sports and touring bikes by the early 1950s. This new choice of machines, combined with the improving financial situation of the time, meant that the 350cc market was in decline as riders availed themselves of the extra performance of the larger bikes. This drop in the 350cc market, combined with the increased demand, especially from the rapidly growing US market, for 500cc bikes and the new and very successful 650cc Thunderbird, led to Triumph dropping the 3T from its range at the end of the 1951 model year. This made good commercial sense. The larger models commanded a higher price than the 3T De-luxe, and the economics of subsequently only producing a number of variations on a single theme must have cut costs. So the 3T De-luxe had to go, not because of any inadequacies but as a sacrifice to the god of profit, and Triumph was not to re-enter the 350cc market until 1957 and the introduction of the Unit Construction Triumph 3TA 'Twenty-one'.

Tiger 85 350cc

The Tiger 85 was the sports version of the 3T De-luxe and, like that model, was initially publicised in *The Motor Cycle* of 8 September 1939. It reappeared in the post-war model range publicity for 1946 and was featured in the full 1947 brochure, but no production bikes ever made it out of the factory. The 1947 brochure described the Tiger 85 as 'a high performance sports machine that will satisfy every requirement of the 350cc class enthusiast'.

The bike was to the 3T De-luxe what the Tiger 100 was to the Speed Twin, a sports version with a mild tune up of the engine and a snazzy new finish. The Tiger 85 took on the Tiger 100 look with its chromed tank with Silver Sheen panels and blue lining, along with Silver Sheen mudguards with a black centre stripe, and the rest of the cycle parts in black. The factory claimed that the lack of production was because the demand for the other bikes in the range was so great, but there were underlying problems. The Tiger 85 featured an 8.5:1 compression ratio, silicon alloy low expansion pistons, and the cylinder head, ports and all moving parts in the engine were highly polished – a similar approach to tuning as done so effectively with the Tiger 100. The engine was claimed to produce 23bhp at 7,000 rpm, but in the Tiger 85's case this led to an unreliable engine unit and there was little that could be done economically to improve it, so it was quietly dropped. Hopwood recounts how the 350 twin had 'weak and flabby' performance that was virtually impossible to improve owing to the fundamental layout of the engine. With its long stroke configuration (bore and stroke were 55x73.4mm), over long flexible pushrods that meant erratic valve control and a crankshaft that was not particularly rigid due to its skimpy clamping arrangements, the Tiger 85 proved impossible to make reliable; the mildly tuned 3T De-luxe was probably as highly tuned as the 350cc engine unit could be and remain reliable.

3TR Trials 350cc 1947

The 3T played a major role in the development of the TR5 Trophy model. When the factory wanted to re-enter competition post-war, the one-day trial events that were very popular at the time were an obvious area to compete in. The Speed Twin and Tiger 100 were deemed too heavy and unwieldy to be competitive in this field, so the 3T was used to form the basis of the 3TR trials bike. The prototype 3TR was a lightly modified standard 3T, with a siamesed high-level exhaust system, 21in front wheel, trials tyres and a wide ratio gearbox. Despite the views of the 'experts' of the time that the single small power pulse per revolution that a twin cylinder engine produced could not compete with the big power pulse every two rev-

The sports 350, the Tiger 85, was never actually put into production. With its paint job based on that of the Tiger 100, with silver mudguards and tank panels, it was a smart looking bike.

olutions produced by a four stroke single, Jim Alves rode the 3TR prototype bike to victory in the 1946 Cotswold Cup national trial on its first outing. He then proceeded to win many more national events. This led to a works trials team, all 3TR mounted, competing in 1947, and the use of alloy barrels derived from the prototype 4-cylinder wartime generator prototype. These bikes produced around 17bhp and were very competitive in the one-day trials competitions. With demand from customers for similar mounts, the factory started work on producing a production version, and according to Harry Woolridge in his book *The Triumph Trophy Bible*, at least one production standard 3TR was produced. However, the factory's decision to compete in the 1948 ISDT meant that an off-road competition bike would have to be very different from the 3T-derived bike. The 3TR in standard form would not be powerful enough to be competitive in the ISDT and there was not much potential

in the design for reliable tuning, so the decision was taken to use a 500cc bike for international competition. Thus the 3TR never made it into production, but did spawn the highly successful TR5 Trophy, which had its frame and running gear closely based on that developed for the 3TR.

Thunderbird 6T 650cc 1950–1962

Introduced in late 1949 for the 1950 model year, the 650cc Thunderbird was developed because of the US market's desire for more performance and less stress. Boring and stroking the Speed Twin engine amply achieved these objectives. The resulting 6T unit produced more power than the existing 5T and Tiger 100 units (34hp at 6,500rpm against the 5T's 27bhp at 6,300rpm and the Tiger 100s 30bhp at 6,500rpm) and, probably more importantly, produced substan-

The Thunderbird was Triumph's first post-war 650cc twin and came in an overall blue finish. This bike has dynamo electrics, as can be seen from the chain case, with the bulge for the crankshaft shock absorber.

With its sprung hub and 650cc iron head and barrel, the Thunderbird made a great tourer with good performance. This late, sprung hub bike has alternator electrics and an SU carburettor.

The sprung hub Thunderbird was a compact, neat machine. The coil is mounted above the distributor in the old magneto position.

tially more torque than the 5T and the Tiger 100, making the engine more long legged and able to pull a higher top gear.

This gave the Thunderbird the relaxed cruising ability and increased performance that the Americans wanted, and also made for an excellent touring or sidecar-pulling unit in the UK market. Even though the Thunderbird followed the Triumph business model of launching a new range with a touring machine rather than a tuned sports machine, the model was launched with a spectacular demonstration of the performance and durability of the new engine.

This comprised three notionally standard bikes plucked off the production line that were ridden down to the Montlhéry circuit in France, where they lapped the track at 90mph (145km/h) for 500 miles (805km) and gave a final flying lap at over 100 mph (161km/h).

The bike's launch was accompanied by extensive advertising of this impressive demonstration of its capabilities. The increased power and torque of the 6T engine necessitated the introduction of a new, stronger gearbox, which was standardised across the range. The cycle parts were identical to those of the Speed Twin, with a rigid frame and the optional sprung hub. Finished in a dark blue (named Thunder Blue) the 1950 Thunderbird was a handsome machine and easily distinguished from the Speed Twin and Tiger 100.

At its introduction the Thunderbird became the top of the range Triumph and since it was relatively softly tuned, with mild cams and a compression ratio of 7:1, its emphasis was on low-down pulling power and flexibility. The Thunderbird's all-iron engine was quiet and refined, but could still pack the miles and do the magic 100mph, as demonstrated by the stunt at Montlhéry. With the relatively low level of engine tune, vibration was not an issue and the bike provided the US market with the long-legged cruising ability it required. In the UK it became a favourite for both effortless touring as a solo and a useful and versatile sidecar lugger. For the first year the Thunderbird was painted in Thunder Blue, but this shade was replaced in the model's second year with the lighter Polychromatic Blue.

In the US the overall blue colour scheme was liked, but there was calls for a change and for the 1953 season the factory produced some Thunderbirds in an

6T Thunderbird Technical Comparison Table

	1950 6T Thunderbird	1956 6T Thunderbird	1961 6T Thunderbird
Engine			
Bore × stroke (mm)	71 × 82	71 × 82	71 × 82
Capacity (cc)	649	649	649
Compression ratio	7:1	7:1	7.5:1
Power (bhp @ rpm)	34 @ 6,300	34 @ 6,300	34 @ 6,500
Carburettor			
Type	Amal 289	SU 590	Amal 376/255
Number	1	1	1
Transmission			
Engine sprocket (teeth/teeth sidecar)	24/21	24/21	22/20
Clutch sprocket (teeth)	43	43	43
Gearbox sprocket (teeth)	18	18	18
Rear sprocket (teeth)	46	46	43
Gear ratios (solo/sidecar)			
Fourth	4.57:1/5.24:1	4.57:1/5.24:1	4.67:1/5.12:1
Third	5.45:1/6.24:1	5.45:1/6.24:1	5.55:1/6.1:1
Second	7.75:1/8.85:1	7.75:1/8.85:1	7.88:1/8.7:1
First	11.20:1/12.8:1	11.20:1/12.8:1	11.4:1/12.5:1
Wheels and tyres			
Tyres, front	19 × 3.25	19 × 3.25	18 × 3.25
Tyres, rear	19 × 3.50	19 × 3.50	18 × 3.50
Front brake	7in (177mm)	7in (177mm)	8in (203mm)
Rear brake	7in (177mm)	7in (177mm)	7in (177mm)
Dimensions			
Seat height	29⅛in (750mm)	30½in (775mm)	30in (762mm)
Wheelbase	55in (1400mm)	55¾in (1416mm)	54¾in (1390mm)
Length	84in (2134mm)	85½in (2170mm)	83⅛in (2120mm)
Ground clearance	6in (152mm)	5in (127mm)	5in (127mm)
Weight	370lb (168kg)	385lb (175kg)	392lb (177kg)
Fuel capacity	4Imp gal (18ltr)	4Imp gal (18ltr)	4Imp gal (18ltr)
Oil capacity	6 pints (3.4ltr)	5 pints (2.8ltr)	5 pints (2.8ltr)

Thunderbirds are Go!

It's a corny title taken from the 1960s' TV puppet show, but it really is appropriate for this description of the Thunderbird launch stunt that, at the time, stunned and amazed the public. Turner wanted to demonstrate the bike's reliability and performance and did this abundantly with a demonstration that included three standard bikes averaging 90 mph for 500 miles around the Montlhéry race track, culminating with a flying lap at more than 100 mph.

Development of the 650cc Thunderbird was in hand during 1949 and several test machines had been running for some time, including the Speed Twins of both Ivor Davis, Triumph's publicity manager, and Neale Shilton, Triumph's South West Region Sales representative. They had been impressed with the performance increase over the Speed Twin; Triumph had been impressed with the new engine's reliability. The company set up a small team for the launch, led by Tyrell Smith and Ernie Nott, and before the ACU observed event, it organised two test runs to smooth the path of the real thing.

The first test was carried out during July 1949 and ended in disaster when the single bike, with chief factory test and development rider Alex Scobie in the saddle, broke a connecting rod after a mere 25 laps of the circuit. The second test, during August, used two bikes, but one bike's clutch burnt out due to the oil level in the primary chain case dropping and then the test had to be aborted by the Dunlop tyre representative after 375 miles (604km) since the left-hand side of both rear tyres had worn down to the canvas. However, valuable lessons had been learned from these tests and the team was ready to return to France in September.

Four Thunderbirds (three for the event and one reserve) were plucked from the production line, lightly prepared in the competition shop and on Wednesday 15 September, ridden down to the Montlhéry track by Neil Shilton, Alex Scobie, Tyrell Smith and Len Bayliss. The four machines met up with Turner in Paris on the way, before proceeding south to the circuit. The following day was taken up with test runs

JAC769 is on display at the National Motor Museum, Beaulieu.

With its all-iron engine and soft state of tune, the Thunderbird was an ideal tourer.

and preparation of the four machines, the team discovering that the bikes had a high-speed misfire. This was tracked down to the production fuel taps not passing enough fuel at sustained high speed, leading to a weak mixture. It was fixed by reaming out the taps. The rest of the team, riders Jim Alves, Allan Jefferies and Bob Manns, along with the Dunlop representative and the ACU observer, Harold Taylor, were flown to France in the Dunlop de Havilland Rapide, arriving on the Saturday evening. Sunday 19th was taken up with further preparations, with the start of the trial scheduled for 9:00 am on Monday 20th. With Bob Manns on bike Number 1 (JAC 769), Alex Scobie on Number 2 (JAC 771) and Jim Alves on Number 3 (JAC 770), the Thunderbirds hit the track and started lapping at between 90 and 100 mph. The only incident was with Number 3 when it came in with a leaking fuel tank, which was replaced with the tank from the fourth machine in under five minutes. This slowed the machine a little, but its average speed was still above the critical 90mph.

After all three machines had covered the 500 miles, they carried out a final flying lap at more than 100mph. The final average speeds for the 500 miles for each bike were 92.48mph (148.83km/h) for Number 1, 92.42mph (148.74km/h) for Number 2, and 92.33mph (148.59km/h) for Number 3. The final flying lap speeds were 100.71mph (162.08km/h), 101.78mph (163.80km/h) and 100.71mph (162.08km/h) for Numbers 1, 2 and 3, respectively. These speeds were telephoned back to Ivor Davis at Meriden, who got the publicity machine working overtime to ensure Triumph's achievement made the press without delay. The day after the run the bikes were ridden back to Meriden where the whole workforce turned out to welcome them home. They were stripped down for inspection by the ACU observer. They exhibited so little wear that he was quoted in the press as saying that all three 'looked capable of an immediate repeat performance'. This was a spectacular end to an impressive feat of endurance.

Triumph used the launch stunt for publicity.

The adverts of the time were evocative and eye-catching.

This 1956 Thunderbird has the swinging arm frame, alternator electrics and classic Triumph looks.

The Thunderbird's nacelle housed the Triumph Rev-o-lator speedometer, ammeter, and combined lights and ignition switch.

all-black colour scheme with gold lining. These, not surprisingly, were (and still are) nicknamed 'Blackbirds' by the punters. The new scheme proved so popular that the importers had to ask dealers to take some standard blue Thunderbirds as demand for black bikes outstripped supply.

One of the defining features of the Thunderbird was Turner's Nacelle. It was fitted to the bike throughout its production life as a Pre-unit model, and it was retained on the Unit Construction version from 1963 until the model's eventual omission from the range in 1965.

The Thunderbird was the top model of the Triumph range, as its largest and highest performance twin, until the introduction of the more highly tuned and sporting Tiger 110 in 1954. However, the Thunderbird remained popular with buyers after the Tiger 110's introduction, since it still fulfilled the requirements of the slightly more mature rider for a refined and comfortable bike with adequate performance. The Thunderbird had the same relationship to the Tiger 110 as the Speed Twin had to the Tiger 100 – two very similar bikes sharing a lot of common components, but

The 1950s' (this is a 1956) Pre-unit Thunderbird was the definitive 'sensible' Triumph, with adequate performance and handling, and a large dose of style.

different enough in performance, specification and styling to satisfy two types of buyer.

The Thunderbird was developed in line with the rest of the Triumph range, but lagged slightly behind the cutting edge. While it always had the sprung hub as an optional extra, it only got the single down tube swinging arm frame in 1955, a year after the T110. With the introduction of the swinging arm frame the overall Polychromatic Blue colour was initially retained, but Polychromatic Grey replaced it in 1956 and the bike gained a black frame, forks oil tank and nacelle, with gold fuel tank and mudguards for 1957 and 1958. For 1959, the fuel tank and mudguards were in Charcoal – a very dark grey and the and the rest of the bike was in black.

The duplex frame appeared on the Thunderbird along with the T120 Bonneville and T110 in 1960. At the same time it gained an alloy cylinder head in common with the rest of the 650s and was graced with the 'Bathtub' rear enclosure and the large 'Roman Helmet'-style front mudguard.

The full enclosure actually made sense on the Thunderbird, since it was still aimed at the mature buyer who actually wanted a sensible, good-performing bike with convenience and weather protection just as important as styling and looks; the Thunderbird was always a good looking bike, even with the enclosures. The tank, front mudguard and 'Bathtub' were finished in Charcoal. For 1961 and 1962 the Thunderbird received a two-tone finish, with black fuel tank top and nacelle, and the 'Bathtub', fuel tank lower parts, front mudguard and fork sliders in silver.

It is worth remembering that Turner's rationale for the enclosure was to produce a bike that was easy to clean and provide good weather protection, and it succeeded in meeting these two aims. However, while the styling obviously reflected Turner's views on motorbikes, he had aged and matured so his views certainly were not shared by many of the younger motor cyclists of the time. This new generation of young riders wanted sporty looks and maximum performance; it was therefore possibly not such a good idea to have the same enclosure on the Tiger 110. The Pre-unit Thunderbird was replaced by a Unit Construction model for the 1963 model year.

The 1956 Thunderbird engine was little changed from when the model was first introduced.

The Thunderbird was produced in a stunning gold finish for 1957.

The Thunderbird received a full enclosure for 1960, with the introduction of the Bathtub.

Tiger 110 650 1954–1961

The Tiger 110 was a logical progression from the 6T Thunderbird and followed Triumph's model development policy of the time – introduce a high performance roadster based on the touring model. However, the Tiger 110 did set a couple of precedents; it used the new swinging arm frame, which it shared with the Tiger 100 while the Thunderbird continued with the rigid frame, from its introduction and its engine was substantially beefed-up. While the crankshaft was still a three-piece bolt-up unit, it was strengthened with larger diameter main bearing and big end bearing journals.

The bike retained the 6T's iron head and barrel, both painted in heat resistant black paint, and the engine output was a claimed 42bhp at 6,500rpm, which was a substantial increase over the Thunderbird's claimed 34bhp. This power increase gave a substantial boost to performance, with contemporary road tests finding a top speed almost matching the model designation, *The Motor Cycle* squeezing 109mph (175km/h) (one way) out of its test machine in 1956.

The new swinging arm frame had Girling shocks with enclosed springs at the rear, and the trademark nacelle sat on top of Triumphs standard telescopic front forks. The wheels front and rear were 19in diameter and the new 8in diameter single leading shoe front brake was fitted with an attractive alloy brake plate, with air intake and extraction scoops for cooling. This brake was housed in a cast iron half-width hub, with an attractively scalloped spoke rim, and nicknamed the 'pie crust' hub. The 4Imp gal fuel tank had the new 'four bar' badge, and was finished in Shell Blue sheen, as were the mudguards.

The 1954 and 1955 Tiger 110 came with a cast iron cylinder head and was similar in appearance to the Tiger 100.

Tiger 110 Technical Comparison Table

	1954 Tiger 110	1958 Tiger 110	1961 Tiger 110
Engine			
Bore × stroke (mm)	71 × 82	71 × 82	71 × 82
Capacity (cc)	649	649	649
Compression ratio	8.5:1	8:1	8.5:1
Power (bhp @ rpm)	42 @ 6,500	40 @ 6,500	40 @ 6,500
Carburettor			
Type	Amal 289	Amal 376/40	Amal 376/40
Number	1	1	1
Transmission			
Engine sprocket (teeth/teeth sidecar)	24	24/21	22/20
Clutch sprocket (teeth)	43	43	43
Gearbox sprocket (teeth)	18	18	18
Rear sprocket (teeth)	46	46	46
Gear ratios (solo/sidecar)			
Fourth	4.57:1	4.57:1/5.24:1	4.67:1/5.12:1
Third	5.45:1	5.45:1/6.24:1	5.55:1/6.1:1
Second	7.75:1	7.75:1/8.85:1	7.88:1/8.7:1
First	11.20:1	11.20:1/12.8:1	11.4:1/12.5:1
Wheels and tyres			
Tyres, front	19 × 3.25	19 × 3.25	18 × 3.25
Tyres, rear	19 × 3.50	19 × 3.50	18 × 3.50
Front brake	8in (203mm)	8in (203mm)	8in (203mm)
Rear brake	7in (177mm)	7in (177mm)	7in (177mm)
Dimensions			
Seat height	30½in (775mm)	30½in (775mm)	30in (762mm)
Wheelbase	55¾in (1416mm)	55¾in (1416mm)	54¾in (1390mm)
Length	85½in (2170mm)	85½in (2170mm)	83½in (2120mm)
Ground clearance	5in (127mm)	5in (127mm)	5in (127mm)
Weight	395lb (179kg)	390lb (177kg)	390lb (177kg)
Fuel capacity	4Imp gal (18ltr)	4Imp gal (18ltr)	4Imp gal (18ltr)
Oil capacity	6 pints (3.4ltr)	5 pints (2.8ltr)	5 pints (2.8ltr)

Early Tiger 110s were handsome bikes, sharing most of their running gear with the Tiger 100.

The front mudguard was a slimline sporting blade, while the rear guard, while still quite slim, was valanced to keep road dirt off the bike and rider. The oil tank and side panel, and the rest of the running gear, were finished in black. With its new swinging arm frame, pokey 650cc engine and proven Triumph gearbox and primary drive, the Tiger 110 was an attractive package, but all was not well. As more power was extracted from the Triumph engine, vibration started to become significant and contemporary reports indicated that it was starting to affect ancillary components. Fuel and oil tanks, and mudguards were prone to cracking and fracture due to the increased level of vibration, and the iron cylinder head could lead to overheating when performance was used to the full. This in turn could result in the head warping or cracking.

Finally, handling was not up to par, with a relatively weakly located swinging arm allowing flex, which could and did lead to wobbles in high speed cornering. Neglecting the swinging arm bushes also lead to rapid wear of the pivot, compounding the handling problems that were replicated on all the swinging arm models. Despite these faults, the T110 was one of the fastest road bikes available and was justifiably popular with the buying public.

The cylinder head cooling problem was inadequately addressed for 1955 with the introduction of an additional vertical cooling fin on the iron cylinder head just in front of each spark plug, but the real problem was the use of cast iron for the head. Otherwise the T110 continued largely unchanged, although the front brake hub was replaced by a hub with a plain spoke rim to overcome problems with the scalloped unit cracking. In 1956 the bike got a new single carburettor, splayed exhaust port Delta cylinder head in diecast alloy. This cured the overheating problems, but was still prone to

The Triumph tank-top rack and nacelle were standard fixtures on early Tiger 110s.

cracking. The head was designed to allow oil to drain from the valve seat pockets into the push rod tubes, so the external drainpipes used on the cast iron head were deleted. Other internal changes included the introduction of shell big end bearings, but the appearance of the model remained very similar to the previous year.

The T110 got a new colour scheme in 1957, with the last years silver sheen being replaced by a bright metallic gold. Along with this change, the fuel tank got chrome 'mouth organ'-type badges. There were no major changes to the mechanicals or the running gear. For 1958, and looking towards the introduction of the Bonneville, the T110 buyer was offered a twin carburettor head as an option. The model took another new paint job for 1958, this time with an overall silver grey fuel tank and mudguards, and everything else in black. Customers were also offered an optional finish with two-tone black over Ivory fuel tank, and Ivory mudguards.

The other main changes were a new full-width hub housing a plain 8in front brake with a plain alloy back plate, losing the attractive air scoop used on the previous years, while the Slickshift gearbox was fitted and bolt on caps were used to hold the front wheel.

Strangely, the front mudguard grew a valance, giving better weather protection, but not looking as sporty as the blade-type fitted previously. The Tiger 110 continued into 1959 with few changes other than a new reversed optional paint scheme of black over Ivory on the fuel tank, with Ivory guards. Then, with the late introduction of the Bonneville in 1959, the T110 lost its role as the sports bike in the range. This was confirmed in 1960 when it received the new full 'Bathtub' rear enclosure and the even larger 'Roman Helmet'-style front mudguard, and 18in diameter wheels. The whole bike was painted in black with the exception of the top of the fuel tank, which was in Ivory, making for a sombre looking model. There were no significant mechanical changes.

The last year for the Tiger 110 was 1961, when its appearance was brightened up with a Kingfisher Blue nacelle, fork shrouds and fuel tank top, while the underside of the fuel tank, the 'Bathtub', the front mudguard and fork sliders were finished in silver.

As the Bonneville had taken over as the sports bike in the range and the 6T Thunderbird was still popular as the tourer, the Tiger 110 no longer had a market to address and was discontinued at the end of the 1961 model year.

The all iron top end on the 1954 and 1955 Tiger 110s was marginal for such a sporting mount. It was replaced with an alloy casting for 1956.

The alloy head on the Tiger 110 improved cooling and gave a boost to performance.

This nice 1957 alloy headed Tiger 110 was at the Amberley Show in West Sussex in spring 2011. Note the 8in half-width front brake.

The major change for the Tiger 110 came in 1960, with the introduction of the Bathtub full enclosure. It was not considered sporty by younger riders.

Bathtubs offered good weather protection and helped make the Tiger 110 a good fast tourer — a task this bike still fulfils today.

TR5 Trophy 500 1949–1959

The TR5 Trophy was introduced to the public at the November 1948 Earls Court motor cycle show, and was included in the range for the 1949 model year. It was a dual-purpose competition machine, designed to compete in the popular sport of trials. This was a test of man and machine, with combinations of road and off-road sections and needed a bike that could handle rough roads and tracks, and still give a respectable performance on the road. The ultimate trials were events such as the Scottish Six Day Trial and the International Six Day Trials, which were major events of the period.

The new Trophy was loosely based on the trials bikes that had been developed from Tiger 100s by the works team in the preceding year to compete in the 1948 ISDT held in San Remo, Italy. In this event the three bikes entered all won gold medals and gained a manufacturer's team award for Triumph. Despite the superb result, Triumph did not rest on its laurels and post-

event analysis showed the Tiger 100-derived bikes to be too heavy and unwieldy. The value of the emerging US enduros market was also recognised and Triumph saw that a production 500cc machine would be competitive in that market as well as in the UK home competition arena. The production TR5 Trophy, although described as a replica of the ISDT winning bike, was really quite different, and had a new frame derived from that of the 3T works trials bikes, which improved handling and cut down weight. The main difference to the 3T frame was the shortened and pushed back front down tube. It was joined to the front engine plates which, in turn, connected to the lower rails.

The engine unit was, in effect, a de-tuned Tiger 100 unit with low compression pistons (6:1) and the defining element was the fitting of an alloy cylinder head and eight fin alloy barrel derived directly from that of the World War 2 generator unit, which improved cooling and cut down weight, and had been fitted to the ISDT bikes. The generator-derived castings included the cast-in lugs for the cooling shroud

Early TR5s had generator engine-derived top ends – note the cast-in, but undrilled lugs on the barrels of this early example.

The rigid TR5's 3T-derived frame gave a shorter wheelbase and better ground clearance than the Speed Twin.

fixing bolts on the side of the barrels, although they were not drilled on the Trophy and the head retained a very squared-off appearance, with the exhaust ports exiting straight ahead rather than being splayed outwards. The sparks were provided from a manual advance/retard BT-H magneto and a dynamo looked after battery charging.

A slim, chromed 2½Imp gal (11.3 litre) fuel tank with silver-painted panels lined in blue and provision for an optional tank rack was specified, along with silver-painted alloy mudguards. The 7in headlamp was equipped with a plug to make it quickly detachable

and carried the ammeter and light switch, and the 120mph Smiths plain, black-faced chronometric speedometer was fitted to the fork top yoke on a bracket. Industry standard 7/8in diameter handlebars were fitted, making the Trophy the only Pre-unit model so fitted.

The wheels were 20in (510mm) diameter front and 19in rear, and fitted with Dunlop Trials Universal tyres; 7in diameter single leading shoe brakes were fitted front and rear. With its rigid frame (although the sprung hub was an optional extra) and the Triumph telescopic forks, the Trophy was a competitive mount

TR5 Trophy Technical Comparison Table

	1949 TR5 Trophy	1950 TR5 Trophy	1951 TR5 Trophy	1955 TR5 Trophy
Engine				
Bore × stroke (mm)	63 × 80	63 × 80	63 × 80	63 × 80
Capacity (cc)	498	498	498	498
Compression ratio	6.0:1	6.0:1	6.0:1	8.0:1
Power (bhp @ rpm)	24 @ 6,000	24 @ 6,000	25 @ 6,300	33 @ 6,500
Carburettor				
Type	Amal 276	Amal 276	Amal 276	Amal 276
Specification	DK/1A, 15/16 bore, 150	DK/1A, 15/16 bore, 150	DK/1A, 15/16 bore, 150	TT type float chamber, top
Number	main jet 1	main jet 1	main jet 1	feed 1
Transmission				
Engine sprocket (teeth)	21	21	21	21
Clutch sprocket (teeth)	43	43	43	43
Gearbox sprocket (teeth)	18	18	18	18
Rear sprocket (teeth)	46	46	46	46
Gear ratios (solo)				
Fourth	5.24:1	5.24:1	5.24:1	5.24:1
Third	7.60:1	7.46:1	7.46:1	6.24:1
Second	12.02:1	11.58:1	11.58:1	8.85:1
First	16.08:1	15.25:1	15.25:1	12.8:1
Wheels and tyres				
Tyres, front	20 × 3.00	20 × 3.00	20 × 3.00	20 × 3.00
Tyres, rear	19 × 4.00	19 × 4.00	19 × 4.00	19 × 4.00
Front brake	7in (177mm)	7in (177mm)	7in (177mm)	7in (177mm)
Rear brake	7in (177mm)	7in (177mm)	7in (177mm)	7in (177mm)
Dimensions				
Seat height	31in (790mm)	31in (790mm)	31in (790mm)	30½in (775mm)
Wheelbase	53in (1340mm)	53in (1340mm)	53in (1340mm)	55¾in (1416mm)
Length	80in (2030mm)	80in (2030mm)	80in (2030mm)	85½in (2170mm)
Ground clearance	6¼in (160mm)	6¼in (160mm)	6¼in (160mm)	5½in (140mm)
Weight	295lb (134kg)	295lb (134kg)	295lb (134kg)	365lb (165kg)
Fuel capacity	2½Imp gal (11.4ltr)	2½Imp gal (11.4ltr)	2½Imp gal (11.4ltr)	3Imp gal (13.7ltr)
Oil capacity	6 pints (3.4ltr)	6 pints (3.4ltr)	6 pints (3.4ltr)	6 pints (3.4ltr)

The TR5's high level exhaust increased ground clearance and helped make it an excellent competition machine.

in trials and enduros, in the UK and the US. It was a classic Clubman's mount, and with full lighting equipment, a siamesed upswept exhaust, silencer on the drive side and trials-type, road legal tyres, the Trophy was fully road legal and could be used as a ride-to-work mount during the week and for competition at the weekend.

The 1950 Trophy gained the tougher 6T gearbox along with revised gear ratios, and a sheet steel crankcase undershield was specified during the season. For 1951 the TR5 unit was harmonised, where possible, with the T100 unit, so it took the close-fin alloy cylinder barrel and a new cylinder head, ending the use of the generator barrel and head. The new barrel had pressed-in cast iron liners and the head had larger inlet valves than the generator unit and splayed exhaust ports. To go with the new barrels and head, new duralumin push rods were specified and the stronger 6T-type connecting rods were also used.

New push and twist filler caps went onto the fuel and oil tanks, and a new exhaust system was needed to fit the new splayed-port cylinder head. These changes resulted in a claimed extra 1bhp and no increase in weight. The TR5 lost its chrome fuel tank in 1952, but had no other significant changes. For 1953 there were

new camshafts with ramps for quieter operation and the engine shaft shock absorber was replaced with a rubber vane unit in the clutch. The main bearings were modified in 1954, and the big end bearings were also increased in size.

The big change to the TR5 came in 1955, with the adoption of the swinging arm frame from the Tiger 100, which meant completely new running gear. The engine also gained T110 camshafts and high compression pistons, marking the change of role for the TR5 from a soft off-road bike to a much more sporting mount, although with the introduction of the 650cc TR6 Trophy, the TR5 would take a back seat to the larger capacity machine, with its greater all round performance. The standard TR5 continued with some minor changes into 1956, but a tuned version, the Trophy TR5R (or TR5/R) was produced in limited numbers (112 were produced with engine frame numbers TR5 76113–TR5 76224 inclusive) in early 1956 to meet the US need for a ready made racer. The engine was tuned using race kit knowledge and had E3134 camshafts, 9.0:1 compression and twin carburettors (although some later TR5Rs had single carburettors), along with a down swept exhaust system with a pair of open megaphones.

From 1951 the TR5 engine gained a close-finned alloy barrel and matching head similar to those used on the Tiger 100.

The TR5R used the standard T100 frame and alloy mudguards, and a TR6-type detachable headlamp was mounted on TR5-type forks. The front brake was the 8in TR6 type and the fuel tank was the small TR5 3Imp gal unit. The TR5R continued to be produced in limited numbers for 1957.

For 1957 the TR5 received the range's new full-width front hub with 7in diameter brake and the more rigid clamp-on arrangement to fix the front wheel in place. The TR5 then continued to be pro-

duced in 1958 with few significant changes, since the TR6 had by then taken over the role of the on/off-road sports model.

The TR5 Trophy's last year was 1959, since that was the final year of the Pre-unit 500cc engine. Only two small batches were made that year, totalling 111 bikes, and these included twenty-six Daytona-specification machines with twin carburettor heads, thirty-six Daytona-specification bikes with standard single carburettor heads and the forty-nine standard TR5 bikes.

The swinging arm-framed TR5 retained many of the off-road features, such as the high level exhaust.

The swinging arm TR5 was a good-looking bike, with good off-road credentials.

Trophy TR6 650 1956–1962

Following on from the success of the TR5 Trophy, it was a logical move for Triumph to put the 650cc motor in the TR5 running gear to create a new model with the minimum of change and development.

Reflecting the US market's obsession with performance and capacity, the new for 1956 TR6 Trophy (also known as the Trophy Bird) looked to be simply an alloy-head 650cc engine in TR5 running gear, and the 1956 and 1957 brochures reflected this, featuring a single picture of an alloy-barrelled TR5 with a reference in the text to a 650cc version.

The new 650cc model had a cast iron barrel, but this was painted silver (in contrast to the roadster's black barrel) to keep the TR5/T100 look, and a single-carburettor Delta cylinder head. The new model was aimed at the off-road competition market that was booming in the USA.

While the TR5 had addressed the on and road sports market with a single model up to the introduction of the TR6 and the swinging arm frame, as time went on the factory saw the need to market two TR6 models, one aimed at road users and one for off-road users.

The first TR6 Trophies used TR5 running gear, but had an iron barrelled 650cc motor. The iron barrels were painted silver to keep up the appearance of the TR5's alloy barrels.

TR6 Trophy Technical Comparison Table

	1956 TR6 Trophy	1960 TR6 Trophy	1962 TR6 S/S Trophy
Engine			
Bore × stroke (mm)	71 × 82	71 × 82	71 × 82
Capacity (cc)	649	649	649
Compression ratio	8.5:1	8.0:1	8.5:1
Power (bhp @ rpm)	42 @ 6,500	40 @ 6,500	40 @ 6,500
Carburettor			
Type	Amal 376/40	Amal 376/40	Amal 376/40
Number	1	1	1
Transmission			
Engine sprocket (teeth)	24	22	21
Clutch sprocket (teeth)	43	43	43
Gearbox sprocket (teeth)	18	18	18
Rear sprocket (teeth)	46	43	43
Gear ratios (solo)			
Fourth	4.57:1	4.66:1	4.88:1
Third	5.45:1	5.55:1	5.81:1
Second	7.76:1	7.88:1	8.25:1
First	11.20:1	11.38:1	11.92:1
Wheels and tyres			
Tyres, front	20 × 3.00	19 × 3.25	19 × 3.25
Tyres, rear	18 × 4.00	18 × 4.00	18 × 4.00
Front brake	7in (177mm)	8in (203mm)	8in (203mm)
Rear brake	7in (177mm)	7in (177mm)	7in (177mm)
Dimensions			
Seat height	30½in (775mm)	30½in (775mm)	30½in (775mm)
Wheelbase	55¾in (1416mm)	54½in (1385mm)	55¼in (1403mm)
Length	85½in (2170mm)	85½in (2170mm)	86¼in (2190mm)
Ground clearance	5in (127mm)	5in (127mm)	5in (127mm)
Weight	370lb (168kg)	393lb (178kg)	390lb (177kg)
Fuel capacity	3Imp gal (13.7ltr)	3Imp gal (13.7ltr)	3Imp gal (13.7ltr)
Oil capacity	6 pints (3.4ltr)	5 pints (2.8ltr)	5 pints (2.8ltr)

The high-level siamesed exhaust helped to confirm the TR6's off-road pedigree.

For 1957 the TR6's compression ratio was lowered to 8.0:1 to aid tractability and it was fitted with a 19in front wheel, replacing the 20in unit fitted in 1956. Larger gauge spokes were fitted to the rear wheel to counter breakages. The Slickshift gearbox was adopted in 1958, along with a new alloy cylinder head with reduced-size combustion chambers and smaller valves.

This new alloy head was found to be prone to cracking, so new pistons with reworked crowns were also fitted. For 1959 the engine received the new one-piece forged crankshaft with central bolt-on flywheel and a 3134 high performance inlet camshaft was fitted. Elsewhere, a froth tower was introduced on the oil tank.

As well as gaining the new duplex frame for 1960, the TR6 came in two variants, the TR6A and TR6B. The TR6A was a road going version, with tachometer (with the drive in the timing cover), road tyres and a low level exhaust system with separate exhaust pipes and silencers, while the TR6B had an upswept siamesed exhaust system with a high level silencer on the drive side. It also featured a Dunlop Trials universal tyre on the front and a Dunlop Sports item on the back.

For 1961 the TR6 came in R and C (Road and Competition/off road) versions for the US market, but was not listed for the UK market. The cylinder head had cast-in pillars between its fins to quieten engine resonances and the frame was strengthened with the additional lower brace from the steering head to the top tube. The frame steering angle was changed from 67 degrees to 65 degrees to improve handling.

The TR6C had twin upswept exhausts with small silencers mounted on each side, with a chevron-patterned heat shield on each pipe to protect the rider's leg. The TR6R had the conventional low level exhaust system.

The final year of the Pre-unit TR6 was 1962, with the TR6 S/S Trophy. This was essentially a single-carburettor Bonneville, with no off-road pretensions. The Slickshift gearbox was no longer fitted and the exhaust system was a low level siamesed affair, with a single silencer on the timing side.

Later TR6s became more road orientated. This is a 1961 UK-market model, virtually a single-carb Bonneville with no off-road pretensions.

The US market continued to take off-road TR6s in the early 1960s. This 1960 or '61 model features siamesed high level pipes that add to its looks.

The timing side of the 1960/61 TR6 Trophy shows the sparse lines of the off roader.

The 1962 TR6 S/S was a road-orientated machine with low pipes.

T120 Bonneville 650 1959–1962

In his introduction to Steve Wilson's book *T120/T140 Bonneville*, Hughie Hancox recounts how, in 1958, the Triumph test department was carrying out extensive testing and putting lots of mileage on a Crystal Grey Tiger 110, nicknamed 'The Monster' because it was equipped with all the parts from that year's high-performance 'race kit', along with a few more goodies and a lot of extra 'know how' from Triumph's talented designers and engineers.

'The Monster' became one of the prototypes of what was to become probably Triumph's most iconic machine, the Bonneville. The latter was being developed following Triumph's well-proven design philosophy – a new model should be softly tuned to uncover any issues that testing has not discovered, then tuned up to produce sportier versions. For the Pre-unit 650s, this process started with the 6T Thunderbird, then the Tiger 110 and now there was a need for an even sportier machine.

Initial development of 'The Monster', basically a Tiger 110 with a twin-carburettor head and some engine tuning, quickly identified the need for a new crankshaft – the old three-piece bolt-up design was beginning to wilt as power levels approached 50bhp. The culmination of this development effort was the T120 Bonneville. The production Bonneville sported a one-piece crankshaft with a one-piece bolt-on central flywheel from the word go, along with the larger main bearings and stronger crankcases introduced in 1954. It proved to be a strong engine, capable of taking the additional power, which at 46bhp was a useful 6bhp over that claimed for the current Tiger 110.

Turner was apparently a little reluctant to approve the bike, but was eventually persuaded that it was ready. Nevertheless, John Nelson, in his book *Bonnie*, tells of how he qualified his approval with the statement: 'This, my boy will lead us straight into Carey Street.' The bankruptcy courts were in Carey Street! The bike was cleared for production in August 1958, which was late in the planning cycle for the 1959 model year, and after the 1959 model year brochures had been printed.

The first 1959 Bonneville featured the single down tube frame and nacelle. Twin carburettors with separate float bowl on a delta alloy head, provided a performance boost over the Tiger 110.

T120 Bonneville Technical Comparison Table

	1959 T120 Bonneville	1960 T120 Bonneville	1962 T120 Bonneville
Engine			
Bore × stroke (mm)	71 × 82	71 × 82	71 × 82
Capacity (cc)	649	649	649
Compression ratio	8.5:1	8.0:1	8.5:1
Power (bhp @ rpm)	46 @ 6,500	46 @ 6,500	46 @ 6,500
Carburettor			
Type	Amal Monobloc Type 376/204 with chopped float chambers and separate Amal GP float bowl, Type 14/617	Amal Monobloc Type 376/233 with chopped float chambers and separate float bowl, Type 14/624	Amal Monobloc Type 376/257 with integral float chambers
Number	2	1	1
Transmission			
Engine sprocket (teeth) (solo/sidecar)	24	22/19	21/19
Clutch sprocket (teeth)	43	43	43
Gearbox sprocket (teeth)	18	18	18
Rear sprocket (teeth)	46	43	43
Gear ratios (solo/sidecar)			
Fourth	4.57:1	4.66:1/5.4:1	4.88:1/5.40:1
Third	5.45:1	5.55:1/6.42:1	5.81:1/6.42:1
Second	7.75:1	7.88:1/9.13:1	8.25:1/9.13:1
First	11.20:1	11.38:1/13.2:1	11.92:1/13.2:1
Wheels and tyres			
Tyres, front	19 × 3.25	19 × 3.25	19 × 3.25
Tyres, rear	19 × 3.50	19 × 3.50	18 × 4.00
Front brake	8in (203mm)	8in (203mm)	8in (203mm)
Rear brake	7in (177mm)	7in (177mm)	7in (177mm)
Dimensions			
Seat height	30½in (775mm)	30½in (775mm)	30½in (775mm)
Wheelbase	55¾in (1416mm)	54½in (1385mm)	55¼in (1403mm)
Length	85½in (2170mm)	85½in (2170mm)	86¼in (2190mm)
Ground clearance	5in (127mm)	5in (127mm)	5in (127mm)
Weight	404 lb (181.8 kg)	393 lb (178 kg)	390 lb (177 kg)
Fuel capacity (UK)	4Imp gal (18ltr)	4Imp gal (18ltr)/3Imp gal (13.7ltr)	4Imp gal (18ltr)/3Imp gal (13.7ltr)
Oil capacity	5 pints (2.8ltr)	5 pints (2.8ltr)	5 pints (2.8ltr)

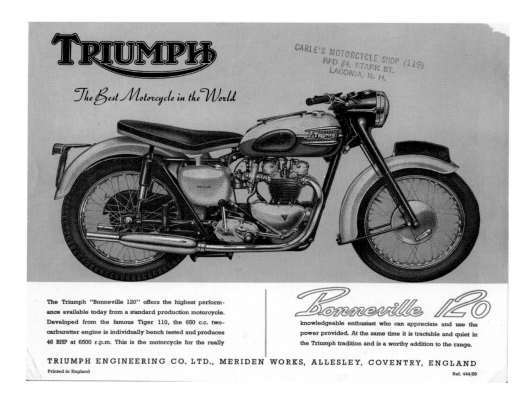

TRIUMPH

The Best Motorcycle in the World

CARLE'S MOTORCYCLE SHOP (119)
RFD #4, STARK ST.
LACONIA, N. H.

The Triumph "Bonneville 120" offers the highest performance available today from a standard production motorcycle.
Developed from the famous Tiger 110, the 650 c.c. two-
carburetter engine is individually bench tested and produces
46 BHP at 6500 r.p.m. This is the motorcycle for the really

Bonneville 120

knowledgeable enthusiast who can appreciate and use the
power provided. At the same time it is tractable and quiet in
the Triumph tradition and is a worthy addition to the range.

TRIUMPH ENGINEERING CO. LTD., MERIDEN WORKS, ALLESLEY, COVENTRY, ENGLAND
Printed in England   Ref. 444/58

The Bonneville was announced after the 1959 brochure had been completed, so Triumph produced a separate flyer.

A separate flyer was therefore produced to provide publicity for the new model. The retail price list issued in September 1958 for the 1959 model year included the T120 Bonneville, but the original print described it as a 500cc Twin and it had to be overprinted with 'ohv twin 650cc'. Naming the model was less of an issue. After Johnny Allen's record breaking run at the Bonneville Salt Flats in 1956, the name Bonneville was adopted for the new sporting flagship. Luckily, since the cycle parts were shared with the Tiger 110 and the engine modifications were not too radical, it was relatively easy to fit the new model into the production schedules.

The first production Bonneville had a strong engine, with its new one-piece crankshaft and bolt-on central flywheel, and including the larger main bearings introduced in 1954, which could cope reliably with the 46bhp it produced. The production engines featured Triumph's famous E3134 cam profiles for the inlet and E3325 for the exhaust, along with 8.5:1 compression ratio pistons. The new light alloy head carried a pair of Amal Monobloc carburettors. These were 'chopped', which meant that the integral float chambers were cut off, and a separate Amal GP (Type 14/617) float chamber was fitted between the two carburettors with a rubber mounting that bolted to the frame at the front of the oil tank/air cleaner assembly.

While the engine of the 1959 T120 was a hot item, the styling was disappointing. The bike shared its gearbox (although it was not fitted with the Slickshift mechanism in recognition of its sporting nature), running gear and 'tinwear' with the T110 and 6T — complete with valanced mudguards and nacelle. The only distinguishing feature was its paint; this was Pearl Grey over Tangerine on the fuel tank, with Pearl Grey mudguards lined in Tangerine. The oil tank of the first production bikes was specified as black, but early on in the run it was changed to Pearl Grey. This colour scheme came in for some criticism from the US market for being a little too flamboyant. The electrical system retained the magneto and dynamo, with a manual advance fitted to the magneto as befitted the sporting status of the bike. US models were offered with the Lucas 'Wader' Competition magneto Type K2FC as an option throughout the life of the Pre-unit Bonneville.

For 1959, T120 Bonneville styling was based firmly on T110 running gear, with touring-style mudguards and the nacelle.

The 1960-on Bonneville had its tachometer driven from the timing cover.

With their slimmer mudguards, separate headlamp, and matched speedometer and tachometer, the 1960-on Bonnevilles had the looks to match their performance.

This 1960 Bonneville is displayed in the National Motorcycle Museum. Note the alternator chain case and magneto ignition.

The 1962 Bonneville featured standard Amal Monobloc carburettors, magneto ignition and alternator electrics.

Original T120 Bonnevilles are fairly common – this one was spotted at the Netley Marsh autojumble in 2009.

Luckily Triumph fixed its styling faux paux in 1960, when the T120 adopted the style already seen on the TR6 – separate chromed headlamp, twin clocks mounted on the top yoke and slim sports mudguards. According to author David Gaylin, the factory was considering fitting the new 'Bathtub' to the Bonneville for 1960, until some stiff lobbying from JoMo's Sales manager Don Brown convinced Turner that this was not what the US market wanted. Combined with the new duplex frame, the styling changes made the Bonneville the bike it should have been on its launch and were gratefully received by dealers and customers on both sides of the Atlantic.

The bike retained the chopped float chamber Amal Monoblocs, but with the float bowl (a standard Type 16/624 rather than the GP type previously fitted) mounted on a threaded rod that was fitted through a metalastic bush on the cylinder head torque stay, to cut down vibration. The Bonneville now also featured the AC alternator which had previously been trialled on the 6T, and to preserve some of the sporting mystique, retained the magneto to provide the sparks, but the K2F unit incorporated an automatic advance/retard unit (note that the US brochure states the model had a manual unit).

The major change for the year was the introduction of the first version of the duplex down tube frame, with the attendant fracture issues that lead to a revised version, with an additional lower top rail, being introduced mid-season. This then led to vibration problems affecting the fuel tank and fittings. The finish was predominantly Pearl Grey, with the fuel tank two-tone and having an Azure Blue lower section. The same colour was used for the centre stripes on the Pearl Grey mudguards. The oil tank and side panel were also Pearl Grey.

The bike continued in this form into the 1961 model year with few changes apart from the colour scheme, which now had the fuel tank painted with a Sky Blue top and Silver lower, and Silver side panels, oil tank and mudguards. The mudguard central stripe was in Sky Blue. A pair of standard Amal Monobloc carburettors replaced the chopped Monoblocs and remote float bowl. The rear wheel was reduced in diameter to 18in, and a fatter 4.00-section tyre was specified.

The final year of the Pre-unit Bonneville was 1962, and with development effort going into the new Unit Construction 650cc machines, the specification of the '62 Bonnie was very similar to that of the '61 machine. For the home market the paint scheme was virtually the same as for the 1961 model, basically Sky Blue and Silver, but the oil tank and side panel were now painted black. The export T120 scheme was changed, with a Flame (red) top and silver lower for the fuel tank, black oil tank and side panel, and silver mudguards, with Flame centre stripe.

After something of a shaky start, the Bonneville became a successful and popular model. Indeed, it came to form the lynchpin of Triumph's success throughout the 1960s.

TR7 Bonneville 650cc 1960

With the Bonneville established as Triumph's top of the range sportster, the US market actually renamed the 1960 T120 as the TR7, a designation based on and designed to capitalise on the sports image of the existing single-carburettor TR6 sports machine. It was also intended to differentiate the 1960 T120 from unsold stocks of the 1959 model, which were by then being sold as a 1960 model. The designation was purely a marketing ploy used in the USA and covered two models – the TR7/A Bonneville Road Sports and the TR7/B Bonneville Scrambler. Both bikes were standard T120s, with T120 stamped on their crankcases. The 'A' was, as the 'Road Sports' designation suggests, a road model with low-level exhaust, while the TR7/B was an on/off-road model with high-level exhaust system a silencer on each side and full road lighting equipment.

T120R and T120C Bonneville 650cc 1961–1962

By 1961 the US market was important enough to Triumph to warrant the production of two distinct types of T120 Bonneville, the T120R for the road and the T120C for Competition – which in the US idiom meant off-road competition. Produced for 1961 and 1962, the two models were based firmly on the T120. The T120R was fully road equipped, with road tyres

and a low-level exhaust system. The main difference from the UK model was the fitment of a Lucas K2FC (red label) auto advance magneto and the obligatory high rise 'US' handlebars. The T120C also had the high handlebars and the K2FC magneto, but in the water-proof 'Wader' form. The T120C model also had a high-level exhaust system, a bolted on steel crankcase shield and Dunlop Trials Universal tyres front and rear. The upswept exhaust system comprised individual exhaust pipes routed over in front of the timing case and primary chain case, and carried short mufflers that ran just above the swinging arm. A short heat shield with chevron shaped cut outs was positioned on the exhaust pipe to protect the rider's leg, but this gave no protection for the pillion rider. With these relatively minor changes to the standard model, Triumph was able to offer its biggest growing market models tailored to the riders' needs.

TRW 500cc 1950 - 1964 (plus 750cc 7ST Prototype)

The TRW was introduced in 1950 as the result of a long and involved procurement process instigated by the British War Department (WD) to define and test a universal military motor cycle during the later stages of the war and in subsequent years.

The basis of the TRW design was the Hopwood-designed 5TW lightweight 500cc side valve twin, designed and prototyped during 1942–43 while Turner was at BSA. However, while this bike was never intended for production, the War Department had begun to formulate a specification for just such a machine, and an initial specification for a universal military motor cycle was issued by the UK's Ministry of Supply in 1946.

The specification called for a bike which would do 80mpg at a steady 30mph, have a top speed of 70mph, weigh a maximum of 300lbs, stop in 35ft from 30mph, have 6in ground clearance, be so quiet as to be inaudible half a mile away, able to ford 15in depth of water and be able to stop and restart on a gradient of 1:2.24. While the specification did not define the engine configuration, boffins at the Fighting Vehicle Research and Development Establishment (FVRDE) at Chertsey, Surry, had privately made it known that

The TRW was the result of a British government procurement to define a Standard Military Motorcycle. Based on Trophy TR5 running gear, it had a 500cc side valve engine.

The TRW featured a four-speed gearbox and a rigid back end. Canvas pannier bags on a steel framework added practicality.

The 500cc side valve twin had alternator electrics. Early bikes had a magneto, later examples had coil ignition.

a 500cc side valve twin would be looked on more favourably than other engine configurations, since it gave the combination of reliability, performance and long life that a military machine needed.

Triumph's competition for contracts to meet this pretty stiff set of requirements came from 500cc side valve vertical twins from BSA and Norton, a 350cc side valve vertical twin from Royal Enfield and a 602cc flat twin, still with side valves, from Douglas, but Triumph won with the TRW. To keep weight down, the prototype TRW made extensive use of light alloys, with Electron used for the major engine castings, while aluminium was used instead of pressed steel for cycle parts such as the fork outer covers, tool box, mudguards and air filter housing. The gearbox appeared to be based on the pre-war unit with a smaller oval outer cover, again probably a weight saving measure. However, when the bike went into production it was closer to a standard Triumph, using mainly Trophy running gear, a standard Triumph gearbox and having a cast iron barrel and alloy crankcases. A prototype TRW is on display at the London Motor Cycle Museum.

Overall some 15,939 TRWs were built between September 1950 and October 1964. As part of the competition to win the contract, two of the prototype TRWs, ridden by Bill Randall and a Sergeant J. Hird, competed in the 1949 Scottish Six Day Trial. Randall won a second-class award and later in the year rode the TRW in the International Six Days Trial (held in Wales), winning a gold medal.

With the setting up of the North Atlantic Treaty Organisation (NATO) in 1949 the TRW was named as one of the standard military motor cycles NATO countries should use and Triumph enjoyed considerable success supplying it to various NATO and non-NATO countries. At home the Army, Navy and RAF, and government users such as the Forestry Commission bought the bike, albeit in relatively small numbers. However, the export market took the majority of production, since the UK armed forces had plenty of bikes left over from the hundreds of thousands delivered during World War Two. Export customers included Canada, France, Sweden and Pakistan.

While the production TRW had a unique engine, the rest of the model was closely based on the Triumph parts bin. The frame was, not surprisingly, the same as that used for the off-road competition-inspired TR5

Trophy. The front wheel was a standard 5T/T100/6T item as was the rear (also shared with the TR5). The fuel tank was a TR5 item, albeit supplied painted not chromed, but surprisingly the standard Triumph tank rack was retained. The front mudguard was the standard steel item with its central rib. The rear was a one-piece unit, like the front made in steel to the standard Triumph ribbed profile, and both were much more robust than the TR5's alloy units. The oil tank was unique to the TRW and the timing-side toolbox was the same as that on the rest of the range. The front forks were the road-type telescopic unit with nacelle, and TR5 springs and road-model stanchions and oil restrictor rod for damping. The gearbox was the standard Triumph unit with the TR5 wide-ratio gears fitted, and the primary chain case, with the front half inner incorporated in the drive side crankcase was unique to the bike.

The electrics were also unique, the bike being fitted initially with a BT-H magneto and alternator. The Alternator provided AC power to the headlamp and a trickle charge to the battery to power the sidelights and the 'dim lights' fitted for convey duty at night. On all models the alternator stator was fitted to the inside of the outer chain case. This had a circular pressed steel cover over the stator that allowed for the all important air gap between the stator and rotor to be checked.

A low level siamesed exhaust system exited through a standard Triumph silencer on the timing side along with a single saddle and pillion pad. To provide carrying capacity, a set of pannier frames was bolted to an integrated rack that in turn was bolted to the rear subframe and mudguard. The frames accommodated canvas pannier bags.

Hence the TRW was a bit of a hybrid, with the unique TRW engine, primary drive and sundry parts (including the electrical system of the early bikes) married to the TR5 frame and a mixture of TR5 and standard road bike fittings, and was referred to as such by the factory. In the press of the day, the bike was claimed to have 80 per cent commonality with the civilian range, and the only part of the original specification the bike did not meet was the weight — the production machines weight about 320lb, not too far from the stipulated 300lb.

The valves were positioned in the front of the engine, driven by a single cam. The tappet adjusters were under the alloy covers on the front of the barrels.

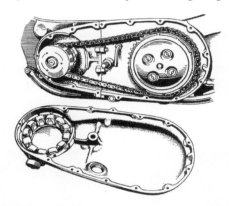

The TRW was unique among Triumph twins, with the front inner of the primary chain case incorporated into the drive-side crankcase casting. The alternator was housed in the outer chain case.

The TRW featured Triumph's trademark nacelle.

The Standardised Military Motorcycle Competition

Triump's competition in producing the Ministry of Supply's Standardised Military Motorcycle came from four post-war British rivals, BSA, Douglas, Royal Enfield and Norton. Strangely, AMC, whose Matchless 350cc singles were well received by the military and riders during World War Two, does not seem to have tendered against the specification. The BSA offering was effectively a development of the model that Bert Hopwood's 5TW twin had been produced as a spoiler for in 1942. Featuring a 500cc side valve, parallel twin engine based closely on the soon to be announced A7, with a single chain driven camshaft and magneto positioned behind the barrels, the bike had telescopic forks and a rigid frame. As on the early A7 twin, the gearbox was bolted directly to the back of the engine, giving it a semi-unit construction. Lightweight frame and running gear were used, based on the A7 chassis. One prototype was built and does not seem to have survived.

The Douglas offering was a 602cc 74mm bore × 70mm stroke flat twin, side valve, known as the DV2 or DV60. This followed the traditional Douglas engine layout and of the three prototypes made, the second had an unusual frame with the fuel tank mounted low down underneath the top frame tube, with separately mounted knee grips above it. The bike gave a claimed top speed of 70mph (113km/h) and 90mpg (3.14ltr/100km). It featured Douglas' unique leading link Radiadraulic forks and one of the prototypes featured torsion bar rear suspension, although the example in the Sammy Miller Museum in New Milton, Hampshire, has a rigid rear end. The only surviving example, this bike also has a more conventional saddle-type fuel tank set up.

The Douglas DV60 was a side valve flat twin.

The 350cc side valve Royal Enfield was a strange looking machine. Girder forks gave it a very old fashioned appearance. This bike is on display at the National Motor Museum.

The Royal Enfield contender was the smallest of the lot, as a 350cc side valve, parallel-twin engined bike. Its most striking feature was the huge combined primary and final chain case, which dominated the drive side and provided lubrication and protection for both chains. The frame appears to be unique to the model and the carburettor was positioned at the front of the engine, between the twin exhaust ports. Old-fashioned girder forks were fitted and the rear end was rigid. One prototype survives in the National Motor Museum, Beaulieu.

The final contender was from Norton, and, like the BSA and Triumph models, it was closely based on the company's proposed post-war twin. A 500cc side valve, parallel twin, it was designed by Bert Hopwood, who by that time had moved from Triumph to Norton. The bike was based on the new 500cc Norton Twin, but with side valves, and featured an alternator in the alloy primary chain case and a single camshaft, chain driven and situated towards the front of the cylinder block. A rigid frame and Norton 'Roadholder' telescopic front forks completed the specification. A single prototype survives in the Sammy Miller Museum.

Three of the contenders, the BSA, Triumph and Douglas, were entered in the Scottish Six Days Trial of May 1948. The BSA, ridden by Sergeant T A Tracy, out performed both the Triumph, ridden by Staff Sergeant J Hird, and the Douglas, ridden by Captain H R Little. The Douglas had to retire on the third day when the engine seized as a result of the oil pump worm drive failing. Despite its performance, the BSA lost the competition for production contracts to the Triumph.

The Royal Enfield sported a huge enclosure for primary and secondary drive chains.

Norton's 500cc side valve twin was attractive and looked very smart in civilian colours. This one is on display at The Sammy Miller Museum.

The TRW was designed to military specification, and is surprisingly
practical in military trim. Large panniers and the hand rack give good
luggage capacity.

There was a single prototype swinging-arm framed TRW. It is now on
display at the London Motorcycle Museum.

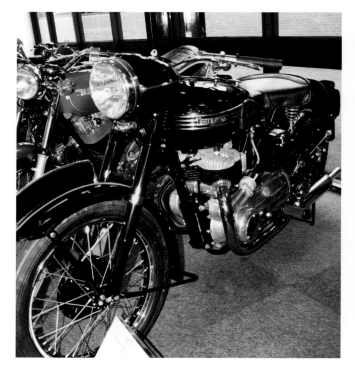

The 750cc 7ST was a TRW-based side valve unit for sidecar use. This
built-up example is in the National Motorcycle Museum.

The layout of the 7ST motor was similar to that of the TRW, but its
appearance differed.

Three marks of TRW were produced over the production run, from late 1949 through to 1964, when construction of the other Pre-unit twins had already finished. The main areas of change between marks was in the electrics, although during the production of the Mark 2 the bike lost its alloy cylinder barrel, which was replaced by a cast iron unit for the rest of the production run.

The Marks 1 and 2 had magneto ignition, BT-H alternators and AC lighting, while the Mark 2B onwards had all-Lucas electrics and coil ignition. The Mark 1 and Mark 2 BT-H alternator supplied AC current to power the headlamp and charged the negative earth battery for the tail and 'dim' lights. For the Mark 2B and Mark 3 models the contact breaker points for the coil ignition were housed in a Lucas distributor that replaced the BT-H magneto behind the barrels, and a Lucas RM14 alternator replaced the BT-H unit.

The output from the Lucas alternator was fully rectified and used to charge the battery, which provided power to all the electrical components, including DC to the headlight. The wiring incorporated an emergency ignition position to enable the bike to be started with a flat battery.

The TRW retained the TR5 type rigid frame throughout its life, and while the sprung hub could be fitted, it does not appear as an option in the 1956 TRW manual. Today there are a surprising number of TRWs in civilian use, both in the UK and abroad, and they make for a pleasant and civilised bike. An article by Fredrick L. Klaiss, *Olive Drab, Or legend of the War Surplus Cycle*, appeared in the July 1973 edition of *Cycle World* and described how he acquired an ex-Canadian Army TRW still in its crate, and how he commissioned and rode it. In addition, many TRWs have been converted into Trophy look-alikes, since their frame is identical to the Trophy's and so is much of their running gear.

Because it was produced to a rigorous specification, development of the TRW was limited, but Triumph did do some experimentation. A prototype of a 750cc variant of the side valve twin was produced, given the designation 7ST and nicknamed 'Jumbo' for obvious reasons.

It was not intended for the military market, rather it was aimed at the civilian sidecar market, which at the time was buoyant. A prototype was built using 6T Thunderbird running gear, including a sprung hub. The engine unit had the same layout as the TRW, with a single camshaft mounted at the front, but with its bore and stoke of 72mm × 90mm the unit displaced a mighty 732cc. The camshaft was chain driven in a manner similar to Hopwood's 1944 machine, and had a distributor sited behind the barrels on the drive side. The distributor was driven by a skew gear taken off the end of the camshaft. The timing cover was abbreviated, covering only the camshaft drive and oil pump, which was driven from the camshaft as on the TRW, which gave an unbalanced look to the timing side. The unit's performance was no better than that of the 500cc unit and the experiment was dropped.

The original prototype is at the London Motorcycle Museum and a second engine, fitted in 1950s' sprung hub 6T running gear, is displayed in the National Motorcycle Museum.

A second development was a swinging-arm framed version of the 500cc TRW. A single factory prototype was produced in 1957, with the standard 500cc TRW engine placed in the new Speed Twin swinging arm frame, with a Trophy type petrol tank. The main problem with the conversion was the distance between the crankshaft and clutch centres.

This was shorter on the swinging arm Triumphs than on the rigid bikes, so the TRW drive side crankcase had to be modified to remove the cast-in front inner chain case, allowing a swinging arm inner case to be used. While the prototype was successful, there was no real demand for the bike from the services so it was not put into production. The prototype survives today and is exhibited in the London Motorcycle Museum.

CHAPTER 3

TECHNICAL DESCRIPTION

The Triumph range of Pre-unit twins that made it into mainstream production can be divided into three distinct engine types, and two types of frame and running gear. Engines comprised the mainstream 500cc and 650cc overhead valve units that were produced through the life of the Pre-unit twin, the less mainstream 350cc overhead valve unit produced from 1946 to 1951 and the 500cc side valve War Department TRW unit produced between 1948 and 1964. Frames and running gear were less complex. Basically there were the rigid-framed bikes, which included the bolt-on sprung rear hub and the swinging arm frames. Frames differed in detail between models, often with changes introduced on one model that would then migrate to the other bikes in the range over subsequent model years.

Throughout production of the Pre-unit twins, Triumph carried out a comprehensive programme of design modification and improvement, leading to many minor and major changes being introduced. These would normally be introduced at the start of a model year. This chapter gives a technical description of each major component that made up the Pre-unit twins and details the major changes made to the components as the models evolved.

The Speed Twin was state of the art at its introduction. This sectioned machine is on display at the National Motor Museum, Beaulieu.

The Engines

The 500cc 5T Speed Twin Engine

Introduced to the public in 1937, the Speed Twin engine was the first in a long line of Turner-designed Triumph twins, setting the basic layout of the majority of the twins that Triumph produced up to the 1980s. It was a vertical twin with the barrels mounted on the top of the light alloy crankcases and with the crankshaft lying across the machine. The crankpins were on a common centre, so the pistons rose and fell together, giving a firing stroke on each engine revolution, making the design a 360-degree crank. Bore and stroke were 80mm × 63mm giving a total capacity of 498cc and with a 7:1 compression ratio the unit produced a claimed 28.5bhp at 6,000rpm.

The crankcases were cast light alloy and the barrel and head were cast iron. Despite this, the original

Speed Twin engine unit was slightly lighter than the Tiger 90 unit and only slightly wider.

The timing side (right hand side) of the engine had a single triangular side cover in alloy. This carried the Triumph trademark triangular patent plate in its centre. These plates were initially brass and carried the Triumph script trademark and the model designation (Speed Twin or, later, Tiger 100) above the various patent numbers that applied to the unit. Under the cover was the gear train for the two camshafts and the Lucas Magdyno. These comprised a half-speed idler gear driven from a pinion on the crankshaft, and then two further camshaft drive gears, inlet at the rear and exhaust at the front.

The inlet camshaft gear also drove a gear that drove the Magdyno, which was mounted on the rear of the engine, below the carburettor. Also under the timing cover was the oil pump. Both the inlet and exhaust camshaft were carried on bushes in the crankcases, and the inlet camshaft drove a rotary breather valve fitted in the drive side crankcase half. The camshafts were carried relatively high in the crankcases and the

The pre-war Speed Twin engine had a cast iron cylinder head and barrel. The barrel was fixed to the crankcases with six studs and nuts.

The Speed Twin engine shared its overall layout with the rest of the overhead valve Triumphs. Note the oil pump, driven from the inlet camshaft.

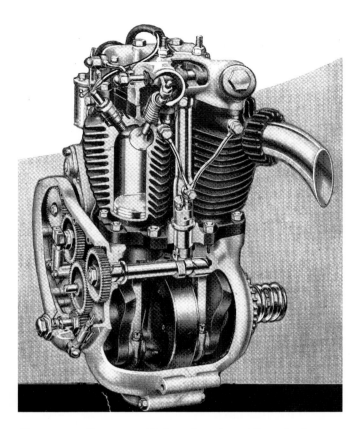

This cutaway of a post-war 5T shows the eight stud fixing for the barrels to the crankcases.

The 5T's bolt-up crankshaft was adequate until the demands for more power of the late 1950s.

use of separate camshafts for the inlet and exhaust meant that it was much easier and cheaper to experiment with different cams to extract more performance, in contrast to the Norton and BSA twins that followed, with their single camshaft designs. Each camshaft had two lobes in its centre that operated on tappets mounted in blocks on the cylinder barrel. The alloy pushrods were short and stiff, giving good control of the valve gear, even at high revs.

The forged steel crank was made in three parts, a central flywheel and two outer pieces. These outer pieces comprised a shaft, a web, a crank pin and a circular flange. Each half's flange was spigotted onto the central flywheel and held in place with six high tensile bolts.

The timing side of the crank carried a drive pinion for the timing gear, and the drive side carried the engine drive sprocket, which incorporated a spring-loaded mechanical shock absorber. The connecting rods were RR56 Hiduminium (an aluminium alloy) forgings, with forged steel end caps.

The big ends were not conventional replaceable shells, but the conrod ran directly on the crank pin, while the steel end cap was lined with white metal that ran on the crank pin. While this gave little trouble in service, it meant that worn big ends had to be fixed with a regrind of the crank and replacement exchange connecting rods, supplies of which have long since dried up. At the time of manufacture, Triumph offered a service to re-metal the bearing surfaces, and some specialist firms can still do this, but most bikes in use today have been converted to use conventional shells, either by machining the existing connecting rods or using later (1956 onwards) connecting rods. The pistons were conventional units with full skirts and two compression and one oil-control ring, and the gudgeon pin ran in a bushed small end eye.

The cast iron barrel had eight cooling fins and a cooling passage was present between the bores. The bores were deeply spigotted into the crankcase mouth, and the base flange of the barrel was fixed to the crankcase mouth with six studs and nuts. The tappets were mounted in separate phosphor bronze blocks front and rear, and the short alloy pushrods were enclosed in chromed steel tunnels — a Triumph twin feature that would be the curse of many owners, since making them oil tight can be a problem. Separate

The 5T's bolt-up crank comprised three components, two crank shaft halves and a central flywheel. Note the large holes in the crank pins that form a sludge trap.

tubes were used to enclose the pushrods to ensure an adequate flow of cooling air between the cylinders, hence the push rod tunnels were made as in as small a diameter as possible to have minimal effect on the cooling air moving between the barrels. The barrel was initially fixed to the crankcases with six studs, but experience with the development of the Tiger 100 led to the use of eight studs for the 1939 engine.

The cast iron cylinder head had separate valve guides and hemispherical combustion chambers. The exhaust ports were splayed outwards and a single carburettor was mounted on the rear on an alloy manifold. The rocker spindles were mounted in separate inlet and exhaust cast alloy rocker boxes. These were bolted onto the head using the inner four of the eight head fixing bolts and another pair of bolts and a pair of studs and nuts under each tappet cover. The round screw-in tappet covers – another Triumph feature made famous, owing mainly to the number that managed to unscrew themselves and become lost – gave access to the screw and locknut tappet adjusters. The chromed steel pushrod tubes butted against the rocker boxes and needed careful sealing to avoid oil leaks.

Drain holes at the base of each valve well in the head, were connected by banjo bolts to drain tubes that led into the pushrod tubes.

The heart of the engine's lubrication system was a brass bodied two-chamber (feed and scavenge) plunger pump, housed under the timing cover and driven by a sliding block from the inlet camshaft. The drive block was the only component (part number E495) that was still used on the last Triumph twins produced. The pump had a spring-loaded ball bearing valve at the base of each chamber, and the scavenge side had a higher capacity than the feed side to prevent wet sumping while the engine was running. Oil was fed from the tank into the pump through drillings in the timing-side crankcase casting. Oil was pumped out through further drillings in the timing cover to the crankshaft end. The timing cover also carried the pressure release valve on its outer cover and a tapping for the feed to the oil pressure gauge and the rocker feed in its front face. Oil under pressure was forced through drillings in the crank to feed the big ends, and then oil splash lubricated the main bearings and bores. The oil drained into the bottom of the crankcases and was sucked up by the scavenge side of the pump and returned to the oil tank. Oil was also fed to the rocker spindles from the take off on the pressure side in the front of the timing cover, and once it had lubricated the top end, drained down from the head into the pushrod tunnels where it lubricated the tappet blocks and camshafts before falling into the sump to be scavenged back to the oil tank.

All in all the Speed Twin unit was robust and reliable, weighed less than the outgoing 500cc single, was slim enough to look like a twin port single and produced a respectable 28bhp, giving a top speed of over 90mph. The only significant change made to the engine pre-war was the switch to eight stud fixing for the barrel to the crankcase in 1938.

Post-war changes

The re-introduction of the Speed Twin after the war saw a number of significant changes to the engine unit. The Lucas Magdyno was replaced by a BT-H (British Thompson Houston) magneto positioned in the old Magdyno position behind the cylinder block, and a new Lucas dynamo was mounted at the front of the engine and driven from the exhaust camshaft pinion.

The engine's breathing system was modified with a rotary breather valve driven from the end of the inlet camshaft and venting out to the atmosphere. The pressure side rocker oil feed from the timing cover was replaced with a feed taken from the return side and fed from a 'T' piece on the oil tank return pipe. This modification cut down the amount of oil fed to the head and meant that the external drain pipes connecting the cylinder head to the push rod tubes could be deleted and replaced with internal drillings in the head and barrel. A revised oil pressure release valve using a spring-loaded piston rather than a ball and spring was also fitted.

For 1946 the engine compression ratio was dropped to 6.5:1 to allow for the very low octane 'pool' petrol available. The engine then continued without significant change until 1949, when the oil pressure release valve incorporated the famous Triumph 'pop out' oil pressure indicator and the compression ratio was raised to 7.0:1. The external oil drain pipes from the head to the pushrod tubes were re-introduced for 1950 to maintain parts commonality with the new 6T Thunderbird unit, and the oil pump was modified to increase oil flow.

More changes arrived for 1951, with a new fully machined crankshaft with a balance factor of 64 per cent, three keyway camshaft pinions, strengthened connecting rods, satellite-tipped cam followers and taper-faced piston rings for quicker running in.

The next major change was the introduction of an alternator for 1953, which meant modified crankcases and the dynamo drive and fixings being deleted. New camshafts with quietening ramps were also fitted. Minor changes to the main bearing were made in the following years and the connecting rods were redesigned to use Vandervell shell bearings in 1956, when the barrel casting was standardised on the 650cc pattern, resulting in repositioning of the barrel fixing studs in the crankcases.

The Pre-unit Triumph had relatively long connecting rods. The early big ends had white metal on their caps and the conrod bodies ran directly on the crank pin.

The final change to the Speed Twin unit came in 1957 when a garter-type oil seal was fitted to the drive side to prevent engine oil escaping into the primary chain case. The final year of production of the Speed Twin unit was 1958; it was replaced by the Unit Construction 5TA unit in 1959.

The 500cc Tiger 100 Engine

After the Speed Twin had been on sale for a year and proved very popular without showing any real weaknesses, it was time for Triumph to branch out and address the sporting end of the market. So the Tiger 100 engine, the sports version of the 5T Speed Twin engine, appeared in late 1938 for the 1939 season and was an immediate success. It retained the overall layout of the Speed Twin and the cast iron cylinder head and barrel, but was lightly tuned to give a claimed 33.5bhp at 7,000rpm as opposed to the Speed Twin's 28.5bhp at 6,000rpm, a useful 17 per cent increase. The engine had a compression ratio of 7.75:1 (up from the Speed Twin's 7:1), achieved using new forged slipper skirted pistons. The engine retained the Speed Twin Camshafts (part number E1485), cam followers

and the cast iron barrel, but the latter was fixed to the crankcases with eight studs and nuts, rather than the 1937 Speed Twin's six fixings, since this had been exposed as a weak point. The 1938 Speed Twin also adopted eight-stud barrel fixing, retaining commonality of parts. The Tiger 100 head and inlet manifold was lightly ported to carry a 1in bore Amal Type 76 carburettor fitted with a short bell mouth, although the valves (inlet and exhaust) were the same as the Speed Twin's. It was claimed that all the moving parts in the engine were polished.

The exhaust pipes and silencers were changed, with the 'cocktail shaker'-shaped silencers sporting detachable end caps that carried the baffles and converted the silencer bodies into racing megaphones when removed. Each Tiger 100 engine was tested on Triumph's Heenan and Froude brake, and the results recorded on a test card that was issued to the buyer of the complete bike. Like the Speed Twin, the bike had a Lucas Magdyno fitted behind the cylinder block, with a manual advance retard mechanism. The basic Tiger 100 unit was used in the post-war Trophy until 1952, when the specifications started to diverge. A bronze cylinder head was offered briefly during 1939 (part number E1710BR) as a performance enhancing

The overall layout of the post-war Speed Twin is shown in this cutaway machine.

The pre-war Tiger 100 engine had an iron barrel with eight stud fixings to the crankcases to cope with its extra power.

Pre-war Tiger 100s had the option of a bronze head for higher performance.

extra for the T100 unit. Bronze is a better heat conductor than cast iron and enabled the bikes to run cooler.

The T100 engine was modified for the 1940 model year, with new full-skirted pistons, a new piston and spring operated oil pressure release valve and modified big ends to increase oil flow through the engine. However, few 1940 model year engines were built and production of the Speed Twin and Tiger 100 units was put on hold until peace came in 1945.

Production of the Tiger 100 unit re-commenced in 1946 and the engine internals were almost the same as the 1940 model; it retained the iron cylinder head and barrel. However, as with the Speed Twin unit, the Tiger 100 had the new timed breather, the rocker oil feed taken from the oil return side and the external rocker box oil drain pipes were replaced with internal drillings. The Lucas Magdyno was replaced with an automatic advance and retard magneto, either a BT-H KC2 or Lucas K2F mounted at the rear of the engine, and a front Lucas 40W dynamo. In addition, the exhaust system lost the removable baffle megaphones. The 1947 model saw no engine changes, but the individual bench test record of the Tiger 100 unit was quietly dropped. The unit continued unchanged until 1949, when the main bearings were modified and the

Triumph oil pressure indicator was incorporated into the oil pressure release valve dome on the timing cover. A number of changes were introduced for 1950, including the re-introduction of the rocker box drain pipes that connected into the push rod tubes, new

Other than its eight-stud fixing for the barrels, the Tiger 100 engine was very similar to the 5T unit.

main bearings and crankshaft, and revised connecting rods with conventional through bolts with lower self-locking nuts.

In 1951 Tiger 100 unit development diverged from that of the Speed Twin when Triumph introduced a light alloy cylinder head and barrel. The Lo-Ex (low expansion) alloy barrel had ten close pitched cooling fins and a natural aluminium finish, making it easy to distinguish from the preceding cast iron barrel, which had eight fins and was finished in black. The cylinder barrel had cast-in steel liners, although these were replaced during 1950 with press-in centrifugally-spun cast iron liners, and for this year the tappet guide blocks were also made from alloy. The alloy head had close pitch cooling fins to match the barrel, external drain pipes from the valve wells and screw-in steel exhaust pipe adaptors that the exhaust pipes clamped on to. The pushrods were made from Duralumin to match the expansion rate of the barrel. The crankshaft was pol-

ished and 6T conrods were used. The compression ratio of the all-alloy engine dropped to 7.6:1. The specifications of the Tiger 100 engine unit and the similar Trophy unit began to diverge significantly from this point.

For 1952, the Tiger 100 unit reverted to the previous cast iron tappet guide and used the 1950-style pushrod tubes with the drain plug bosses, but the TR5 Trophy unit continued to use the alloy tappet blocks. An 8:1 compression ration option was offered for the US market.

Three versions of the T100 unit were produced for 1953, the T100 road unit, the TR5 on/off-road and the T100C for competition. The T100C had a twin-carburettor alloy head with parallel inlet tracts, racing profile cams (the well-known E3134 profile), and the standard T100 and TR5 gained new E3275 camshafts during the year in a successful attempt to quieten the valve gear. The T100 and the US market T100C both had an 8:1 compression ratio.

The Triumph Twin engine used gears to drive the twin camshafts. This is a Tiger 100 with a dynamo drive at the front and a magneto drive to the rear.

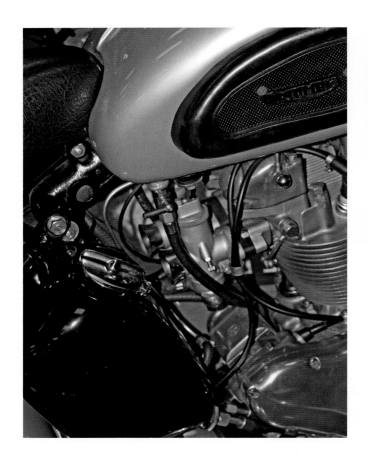

TOP LEFT: The post-war high performance option for the Tiger 100 was the alloy twin carburettor head.

ABOVE: The close-finned alloy barrel fitted to the Tiger 100 looked good and helped the engine run cooler.

BELOW: Later Tiger 100s had an alloy close-finned barrel and single carburettor alloy cylinder head.

There were major changes with the introduction of the swinging arm models in 1954, with the T100 featuring a new crankshaft with larger diameter big end journals (15/8in/41mm in diameter), strengthened connecting rods and a new sludge trap tube in the crankshaft. The twin-carburettor head seen on the previous year's T100C was an option.

For 1955 the home versions had the US-market 8:1 compression ratio and the new Amal Monobloc carburettor was fitted to single-carburettor models. Vandervell shell-type bearings were fitted to 1956 models.

The 'Delta' light alloy splayed twin carburettor head was introduced as an optional extra for the 1957 T100, along with a number of engine changes to go with it. The Delta head is also referred to as the 'HDA' head, HDA standing for High Duty Alloys, a firm that specialised in the forging and casting of alloy components. The Delta head was made from Hiduminium, an aluminium alloy developed by Rolls-Royce in the 1930s that had high strength and could withstand high temperatures. It was often used in high performance aircraft pistons. The head featured splayed inlet ports, giving rise to the description 'Delta Head' and carried two Amal Monobloc carburettors and larger inlet valves. The valve springs were racing pattern, and the area around the valve springs was remodelled to allow oil to drain directly into the push rod tubes, allowing the deletion of the external oil pipes. The valve guides were in bronze. Bikes fitted with the Delta head also had the engine modified to give a compression ratio of 9:1 and the cams were E3134 profile with associated followers.

The 1958 season saw the drive side garter sear seal fitted to the crankshaft and for 1959, the final year of production, the T100 was fitted with a new one-piece crankshaft with bolt-on flywheel, as fitted to the T120 Bonneville. Designed to cope with the power developed by the Bonneville unit (essentially a twin carburettor T110 engine), this new crankshaft finally replaced the 1930s' three-piece bolt-up crankshaft. It was more rigid and could take much more power than the previous unit. It also sported large 15/8in diameter big end journals and new connecting rods to match.

The T100 flywheel was 2½in (63.5mm) wide and had a balance factor of 50 per cent. The following year saw the Pre-unit T100 being replaced by the Unit Construction T100A model.

The 650cc 6T Thunderbird Engine

The 6T engine, introduced in September 1949 for the 1950 model year, was, in essence, a bored and stroked Speed Twin designed to meet US market needs. With a bore and stroke of 71mm × 82mm (the speed Twin was 63mm × 80mm) the 6T unit had a capacity of 649cc, neatly fitting in the 650cc class. The increase in bore meant that a new barrel casting was needed to keep enough meat on the bores, but the 2mm increase in stroke meant that virtually the same crankshaft as used on the 5T could be used.

The 6T unit followed the successful Speed Twin layout with cast alloy crankcases, and a cast iron head and barrel. The crankshaft was a three-piece bolt-up unit with a central flywheel. The plain big end bearings were formed from the Hidiminium conrods running directly on the crank journals along with the white metal fused directly on the their steel end caps. New, stronger connecting rods were fitted, as RR56 light alloy 'H'-section stampings and were very similar in design to those used in the GP engine. As in the T100 rods, the forged steel end caps were white metal lined, while the rod eye ran directly on the big end journal. Ball bearings supported the crank in the cases. The fore and aft camshafts were gear driven on the timing side and the BT-H magneto was flange mounted behind the barrels and driven off the inlet camshaft pinion. The front-mounted Lucas dynamo was driven off the exhaust camshaft pinion.

A plunger oil pump was driven from the inlet camshaft and pumped oil directly into the end of the crank, where it fed the big ends. Alloy rocker boxes sat on the cast iron head and the rocker oil feed was taken from the oil return feed. Oil from the top end drained into the sump through external drain pipes from the head to the push rod tubes, in a system similar to that seen in the pre-war 500cc engine unit. The 6T unit produced 34bhp at 6,000rpm and with its much higher torque was able to take higher gearing than the Speed Twin.

Once introduced, the 6T unit underwent detailed development in line with the other engines in the Triumph range, but most of the changes were minor, showing how right the engine was from the word go. The 1951 engine saw the timing side main bearing changed to a roller bearing and the tappets were Stellite tipped to combat wear.

The 650cc 6T Thunderbird engine had a cast iron head and barrel like the 5T.

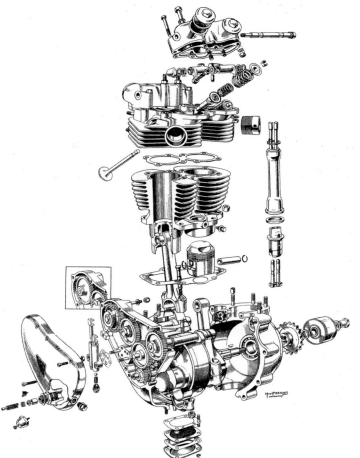

The Triumph 6T 650cc engine had a cast iron barrel and head and was identical in layout to the 500cc units.

The engine was equipped with the SU-type Constant Velocity (CV) Carburettor from the 1952 model year through to the 1958 model year, giving excellent fuel economy without compromising performance.

Quietening ramp camshafts (E3275 type) were fitted during 1953, while the introduction of an alternator for 1954 resulted in a new crank and cases, with larger diameter big end journals and new main bearings. Despite the introduction of the swinging arm frame for 1955, the main engine change was the introduction of a sludge trap to the crankshaft and the fitting of the then new Amal Monobloc carburettor. For 1956, Vandervell steel-backed big end shells were fitted, meaning new connecting rods and easier overhauling.

The next major change was in 1959, with the introduction of the new one-piece crankshaft with its bolt-on flywheel, and in 1960 the brass-bodied oil pump was replaced with an aluminium-bodied unit. After these few years of relatively few modifications, for 1961 the 6T was subject to a number changes to bring it into line with the rest of the Triumph range. An alloy cylinder head was fitted, along with sports camshafts as used in the Tiger 110 (E3325) and, later in the year, E4220 camshafts were installed along with a slightly wider flywheel.

The following year, 1962, was the last one for the 6T before it was replaced by the Unit Construction 6T, but it still took the new crankshaft fitted to the rest of the 650cc range, with pear-shaped crank webs. The aluminium oil pump had proven troublesome in service as heat caused the bodies to expand, giving a corresponding drop in oil pressure, so a cast iron-bodied pump was substituted.

The 650cc Tiger 110 Engine

The Tiger 110 unit was derived from the Thunderbird 6T unit and introduced for 1954 along with the swinging arm frame. The T110 retained the 6T's cast iron cylinder barrels, but had a modified head, still in cast iron but with modified porting and larger inlet valves for better breathing. It also featured a beefed-up crankshaft with larger diameter journals and stronger main bearings, and E3325 camshafts, as used on the TR5 unit. This cam profile was based on the 'Q' cams

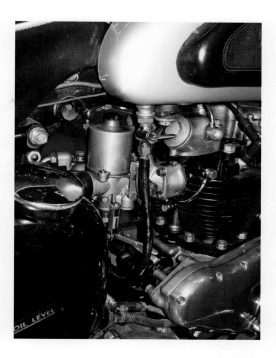

The 6T Thunderbird was fitted with an SU constant velocity carburettor from 1952 to 1958. The SU gave excellent fuel economy and smooth running.

The SU carb was a tight fit on the 6T unit, but worked well.

The sporting T110 was initially fitted with an iron head, which could crack or cause overheating.

developed for racing by the US distributor. With a compression ratio of 8.5:1, the engine gave some 42bhp at 6,500rpm. Unlike the Thunderbird and 5T, which had the new fangled alternator fitted, the T110 was fitted with a dynamo and manual advance magneto, as was the T100.

A new iron head was produced for 1955 with an extra cooling fin that improved matters but did not completely solve the overheating issue; for 1956 the overheating problem was put to bed with the introduction of an alloy head. This was designed with a common area for each pair of inlet and exhaust valves, with the pushrod tunnels mating to this part of the head, rather than to the rocker boxes as in previous years. This redesign allowed excess oil to drain down directly into the pushrod tubes, which meant that at long last the external oil drain pipes from the head could be deleted for good. The compression ratio

stayed at 8.5:1. The head was prone to cracking between the spark plug hole and the stud holes, however, a problem that would only be fixed with the nine-stud head introduced on the Unit Construction twins in 1963.

Home market compression ratio was reduced back to 8:1 in 1957 and an optional tachometer was listed, driven from the timing cover. A twin carburettor head was offered as a T110 option for 1958 and both it and the single carburettor head were modified in attempts to solve the cracking problem, but with limited success.

In 1959 the T120 Bonneville engine was introduced and all the 650cc bikes shared the new, much stronger, one-piece crankshaft with the flywheel secured to it by radial bolts. All the 650s got the alternator electrics in 1960, and the T110's magneto was an automatic advance type. From 1960, T110 development took a back step to that of the T120. The final year for the

The alloy head, as fitted to the later Tiger 110s, was an improvement.

T110 was 1961, with the engine receiving a revised cylinder head with cast-in webs between the fins to cut out resonances. The Triumph road sports mantle was taken on by the T120 in 1962, the last year of production of the Pre-unit bikes.

The 650cc T120 Bonneville Engine

The Bonneville engine represents the epitome of the evolution of the production Pre-unit Triumph engine. In many ways it was a logical extension of what had gone before and took the best parts of the 500cc and 650cc units to give the ultimate performance unit. Probably the most important part of the puzzle that contributed to the evolution of the T120 Bonneville unit was the one-piece forged crankshaft, which was readied for the 1959 model programme. However, when the 650cc 6T Thunderbird unit had been introduced in 1950, it marked the first step in increasing the Speed Twin unit's capacity, and while it produced more power than the 5T and Tiger 100, it still retained the basic architecture and build of the smaller unit.

While the 6T was tuned more for mid-range power and torque, the sports derivatives, the TR6 and, more importantly, the Tiger 110, were more highly tuned and produced more power at higher revs, in response to demands from the home, but particularly the US market, for greater power and increased performance.

This continuous drive for performance led to reliability issues and racing the larger bikes soon showed that the three-piece bolt-up crankshaft, even with the larger diameter big end journals and main bearing introduced in 1954, was approaching the limits of the power that it could handle. The answer was to produce a one-piece crank that fitted through a separate flywheel, with a precision ground face between the two. The flywheel was then fixed in place with three radially positioned 7/16in (11mm) diameter bolts. This gave a strong, rigid structure that could handle the

The defining element of the 1959 650cc T120 Bonneville engine was its twin carburettor head.

The 1959 Bonneville was fitted with 'chopped' Amal Monobloc carburettors with a separate float bowl rubber-mounted between them.

Later T120 Bonnevilles had conventional Amal Monobloc carburettors. Note the tachometer drive, taken from the end of the exhaust camshaft.

increased power being wrung from the tuned T110 units and looked to be reliable enough to justify an even higher-powered unit than the T110 for road use.

This new crank could take the power generated by tuning the T110 and in a test unit, built with a Tiger 100 Delta-inspired, splayed port, all alloy twin-carburettor head; E3134 camshafts; and 8.5:1 pistons, the engine gave 48.8bhp. Development continued with this twin carburettor T110 and the engine specification of the T120 was eventually finalised with E3134 inlet and E3325 exhaust cams, twin 1¹⁄₁₆in (27mm) diameter splayed inlet ports on the alloy head, cast iron barrel, new one piece crankshaft with 85 per cent balance factor and twin 1¹⁄₁₆in (27mm) Amal Monobloc carburettors with the float bowls and with a remote Amal GP float chamber rubber-mounted between them.

The engine had the manual advance/retard magneto and dynamo fitted in the standard Triumph positions at the front and rear of the unit. The production unit produced a claimed 46bhp at 6,500rpm. For 1960 the T120 unit received an auto advance/retard Lucas K2F magneto and a Lucas AC alternator driven from the drive side crankshaft, so the dynamo drive was deleted.

The chopped Monoblocs and remote float bowl were replaced by standard Amal Monoblocs with integral float chambers in 1961, and for 1962 the engine gained a new crank with pear-shaped side cheeks, along with a new central flywheel. The final year of Pre-unit T120 production was 1962; it was replaced by the Unit Construction T120 for the 1963 model year.

The T120 Bonneville had alternator electrics by 1961, but retained the magneto.

The 500cc TR5 and 650cc TR6 Trophy Engines

The production TR5 engine was introduced for the 1949 season and was, broadly speaking, closer to the Tiger 100 than the Speed Twin in specification. The TR5 Trophy unit, introduced as a production model in 1949, was based on the T100 unit and very similar in specification. The main difference was the use of the alloy cylinder and barrel from the generator motor, which were used to make the engine lighter and for better cooling. Valve diameters were the same for inlet and exhaust at 15/16in (24mm) and the engine had a low compression ratio of 6.0:1 to give good low down 'grunt'.

The TR5 unit gained the Tiger 100's close-pitched fin barrel and new Delta alloy cylinder head for 1951, with the larger inlet valves at 17/16in, while the

exhaust valves remained at 15/16in and 6T conrods, while the compression ratio remained unaltered.

The TR5 engine received new camshafts with quietening ramps in 1953 and a larger timing side main bearing and big end journals for 1954. Sports camshafts and 8.0:1 compression-ratio pistons were fitted in 1955, and for 1956, shell big end bearings were fitted. The TR5 engine then only saw detail changes before being discontinued at the end of the 1959 model year.

The TR6 Unit

The TR6 Trophy engine was introduced in August 1956 and was based on the 650cc 6T Thunderbird unit, but tuned and fitted with an alloy cylinder head. It retained the 6T iron barrel, but this was painted

Early TR5 Trophy engines had an alloy head and barrel based on the generator engines produced in World War Two. These units retained the cast-in lugs used to attach cooling shrouds to the stationary engines, but they were undrilled.

The TR5 Trophy gained the new close-finned alloy head and barrel in 1951. This barrel was also fitted to the T100 in 1951.

The generator engine castings mark this TR5 out as an early example.

silver to give it the appearance of alloy and link it to the TR5 unit.

The 71mm × 82mm unit had a relatively high compression ratio of 8.5:1 and a sports camshaft. It gave a healthy 42bhp at 6,500rpm. For 1957 the compression ratio was reduced to 8.0:1, but claimed power remained at 42bhp. For 1958, the TR6 had a new cylinder head with reduced diameter combustion spheres and for 1959 it had the one-piece crankshaft. New crankcases without the dynamo drive arrived in 1961, and the cylinder head had cast-in pillars between the fins to reduce noise from fin resonance. The final year of the Pre-unit TR6 engine was 1962, when the engine's balance factor was changed, requiring a new crankshaft bob weight shape. By 1962 the TR6 unit was very much a single carburettor Bonneville.

TOP LEFT: The TR6 Trophy barrels were cast iron, but painted silver by the factory.

ABOVE: Later TR6s received flamboyant paint schemes that were in demand in the USA at the time.

LEFT: The TR6 engine was a tough and reliable unit, despite its cast iron barrel.

The 350cc 3T and Tiger 85 Engine

The 3T engine shared its overall layout with the Speed Twin unit. It was a long stroke unit with a bore and stoke of 55mm × 73.4mm, giving a capacity of 349cc. It featured a number of significant changes that reflected the lower performance expected from a 350cc unit.

The 3T's one-piece cylinder head shared its design with that of the wartime 3TW head – indeed both engines were developed at the same time – and was very similar in appearance. Produced in cast iron, the engine's relatively complex one-piece casting included the rocker boxes and carried the rocker shafts, which eliminated the need for the separate bolt-on rocker boxes seen on the larger capacity bikes' head. This improved oil tightness and the head also gave excellent access for adjusting valve clearances through the provision of large oblong openings front and rear. The rocker box covers, one for inlet and one for the exhaust, were alloy and held in place by a single cen-

tre stud with a large knurled nut allowing removal without any tools. The cast iron cylinder barrels followed the practice of the larger engines, with a cast-in gap between the cylinder bores and separate push rod tubes front and rear.

There were two distinct sets of barrel and head fixings used on the 3T, described by Triumph as the '1st Condition' and '2nd Condition'. The 1st Condition fixings were used from 1946 and used eight long studs between the crankcase and the head. The studs screwed directly into the cases and the barrel was fitted over these studs. The top of the studs had threaded inserts that the eight head bolts screwed into, clamping the head and barrel together. The cylinder head gasket for the 1st Condition comprised a pair of rings that fitted over the raised spigot on the barrel. The 2nd condition fixings used from 1947 mimicked the larger twins' fixing method, with eight short studs and nuts to hold the barrels to the crankcases and eight bolts screwed into threaded holes in the barrel to hold the head in place. The head gasket for the 2nd Condi-

The 350cc 3T engine unit was visually similar to the 5T, but had a one-piece head with no separate rocker boxes and a different crank design.

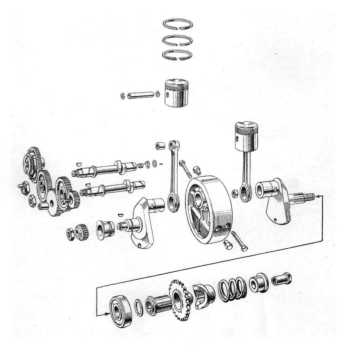

The 3T's crank was a clamp-up affair, which was not particularly stiff. While it coped in the softly tuned 3T, it was too weak for the Tiger 85, which did not enter production.

The 3T crank was weak, but with its long stoke it was tractable, if not a high revver.

tion unit was a one-piece copper item similar to that used for the larger twins.

The bottom end also differed significantly from that of the larger models. The 3T crankcases were cast alloy components, with a pair of camshafts positioned high in the cases and driven by gears. The plunger oil pump was driven by a sliding block off the inlet cam and the unit had a front mounted dynamo and rear mounted magneto, also driven from the relevant camshaft pinion, so far just like the larger models. However, the 3T crankshaft and main bearings were different to those of the larger models, but similar to the 3TW and TRW units. The crankshaft ran on a roller main bearing on the drive side and a bush on the timing side. Oil was fed through the bush to give a pressure feed to the big ends. The 3T crank comprised three parts. On each side there was a one-piece crank half, which had a combined main shaft, crank cheek and big end journal, and a central flywheel. Each crank half big end slotted into a hole in the central flywheel and both were located and secured in place using precision ground high-tensile bolts. This allowed

for the use of one-piece connecting rods made from high tensile alloy steel with white metal big ends, with the bearing material deposited directly onto the conrod eye. The small ends were bushed and the pistons were alloy.

The crankshaft construction was the engine's biggest weakness, probably followed by its long stroke. The crank was not as strong or rigid as that used on the larger twins and while it performed satisfactorily in the relatively softly tuned 3T, with its mild 17bhp at 6,000 rpm, when it was asked to give the 23bhp at 7,000 rpm needed for the T85, it wilted and proved to be inadequate for the job. During T85 testing it became apparent that crank flexing was occurring, leading to main and big end bearing failures, and this was cited as the main reason the T85 never made it into production.

The failure of the T85 showed that the 3T unit had little scope for development, and it remained broadly unchanged after the introduction of the 2nd Condition barrel fixings in 1947. The model was discontinued at the end of the 1951 model year.

The timing side of the 3T shared the Triumph family look, with only the one-piece cylinder head with its integral rocker boxes looking different to the larger models.

Despite being the economy model of the range, the drive side of the 3T still sported a handsome alloy primary chain case.

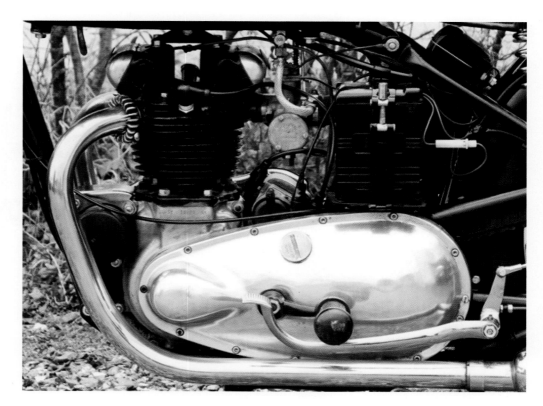

The 500cc TRW Side Valve Engine

The TRW engine was unique among Turner's production Triumph twins as a side valve unit. A side valve was favoured by the military since it offered soft power characteristics and the configuration was simpler to produce and maintain. The military also stipulated that the engine should be inaudible at a distance of half a mile and the side valve configuration could be made much quieter than an overhead valve design. Other features unique to the TRW included a single camshaft sited at the front of the engine and the use of an AC alternator in the primary chain case from the start of production. The drive side was also different to that in the rest of the range, since the front half of the inner primary chain case was cast in one piece with the drive side crankcase. This had a vertical face at its rear and a separate rear inner case was bolted to it using four studs. An attractive alloy outer case covered the lot. The engine had a bore and stroke of 63mm × 80mm, displacing 499cc, and with a 6.0:1 compression ratio it produced 16.8bhp at 5,000rpm.

The bottom end of the engine used many features already employed on the 3T unit. The alloy crankcases were cast from DTD.424 aluminium alloy and the crank's main bearings comprised a ball race on the drive side and a white metal plain bearing on the timing side. Oil for the big ends was fed through this bearing. The crank was a three-piece clamp-up unit, similar to the 3T's, with two crank halves, each comprising a main shaft and a big end journal, clamped to the central flywheel using two high-tensile steel alloy bolts. As the unit produced about the same power as the 3T, the crank design proved to be adequate for the TRW. The connecting rods were forged alloy units in RR65 Hiduminium. These were one-piece units without the bolt on end caps as used on the 500cc and 650cc overhead valve twins, and had pressed in circular white metal-on-steel big end bearings. The 'Lo-Ex' alloy pistons had two compression and one oil control ring and ran on phosphor bronze small end bearings. The timing-side crankshaft end carried the engine pinion and a large diameter idle pinion drove the forward mounted camshaft pinion and the rear magneto

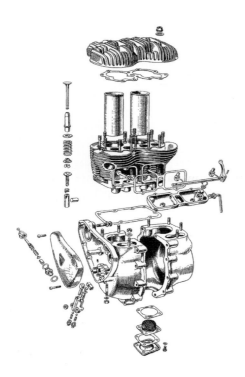

The TRW was a side valve twin. An iron barrel with apertures in the front gave access to the tappets.

The TRW engine's crankshaft was similar in design to the 3T unit. A single camshaft was located at the front of the engine.

The TRW kept the Triumph look and trademark timing cover. An alloy head aided cooling.

Later TRWs were equipped with points ignition, with a distributor mounted behind the barrels. This model sports a non-standard Amal Concentric carburettor.

or distributor pinion. The oil pump was the standard Triumph plunger unit, repositioned to the front of the case where it was driven by a sliding block from the camshaft pinion nut. On the drive side, a single-row chain was driven by a sprocket splined onto the crank end and outboard of the sprocket was the rotor for the alternator. Since the alternator left no room for the engine shock absorber, a rubber vane-type was incorporated in the clutch.

The barrel was a single casting in DTD.324 aluminium alloy for the Mark 1 and early Mark 2 units, but the material was changed to cast iron on later Mark 2s and all Mark 2B machines. The alloy blocks had pressed-in, close-grained cast iron liners and these had to be replaced when worn. The cast iron blocks could be re-bored twice to +20 and +40 thou, and new oversize pistons were available. Both types of barrel casting had the valves and tappets housed in the front of the block and there were two rectangular hatches on the front of the barrel to give access to the tappets. A single alloy cover closed the tappet hatch, and also carried the engine breather and the valve

lifter, which operated on both the exhaust valves. This cover was held on by two studs and located using dowels. A simple spring-loaded ratchet mechanism was used to adjust the valves, using a special spanner provided in the tool kit. The spanner fitted to a spigot between each pair of valves, which engaged with a 'gear' on the side of the adjuster at the bottom of the spring. By pivoting the spanner the adjuster was moved up or down and each ratchet would give about twenty-five thou of adjustment to the tappet.

The carburettor was a Solex Type 26 WH-2, horizontally mounted on the rear of the block. It had a butterfly-type throttle as favoured by the military; research had shown that the slides in the then-current Amal carburettors could and did jam, or stick, in the typical conditions encountered by these machines in their military role. A choke function was provided by a separate lever-operated starter jet, rather than a conventional cable-operated air intake restrictor, again to survive military conditions. The carburettor fed into a circular inlet manifold at the rear of the cylinder block, which changed shape to oval, but

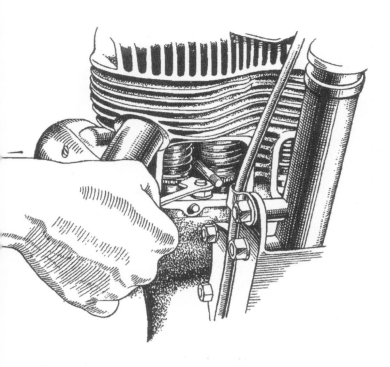

Tappet adjustment on the TRW was by click stop adjusters housed in the front of the barrel.

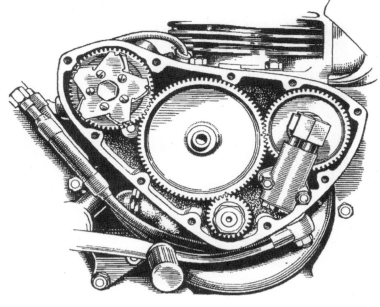

The TRW timing chest had a large idler wheel to drive the front-mounted camshaft and the magneto or points distributor to the rear.

retained the same cross sectional area as it passed between the two bores. Turner also claimed that this feature assisted cooling as well an imparting just enough warming to the incoming fuel air mixture. After passing between the bores, the inlet track split to feed each individual cylinder.

The one-piece cylinder head was cast in DTD.324 alloy like the earlier barrels and was heavily finned to assist cooling. The spark plugs were located above the exhaust valves. Lubrication was dry sump, as usual Triumph practice, and the plunger pump fed oil though drillings in the timing side crankcase to the timing side main bush, where it made its way to the big ends via more drillings. A sludge trap was fitted in the crankshaft to catch any particles in the oil. Oil then dropped to a small sump at the bottom of the crankcases, where the scavenge side of the oil pump returned it to the oil tank via a pick-up. The camshaft, pistons and timing gears were lubricated by splash from the oil that had been fed to the big ends. Oil pressure was indicated by

the Triumph pop-out indicator on the rear face of the timing side. In line with the rest of the range, relatively crude oil filtration to supplement the sludge trap was provided by a gauze filter on the sump and a second gauze filter on the oil tank feed.

The Mark 1 and Mark 2 TRW engine units were fitted with a BT-H magneto, type KC.2-S4 and a BT-H AC alternator. The magneto was an anti-clockwise unit (ie. the magneto rotated anticlockwise when looked at from the points end), unlike the magnetos fitted to 'normal' Triumph twin engines, since it was driven directly off the large timing pinion, itself driven directly off the crank. The Mark 2B machines lost the magneto and gained coil ignition, with a distributor replacing the magneto, and had a Lucas alternator to power a DC-based positive earth electrical system. The engine, while different to the standard Triumph overhead valve motor was a useful and gentle unit that served the various forces it was supplied to reliably for many years. Indeed, it is still sought after today.

A valve lifter was possibly a bit of overkill, bearing in mind the low compression ratio.

The TRW was equipped with an alternator in the primary chain case.

Gearbox and Primary Drive

The early Speed Twin, Tiger 100, and 3T shared the same design of gearbox, which was the same as that fitted to the Tiger 90, albeit with changes to the internal gear ratios for the various models. It was an alloy-cased four-speed unit with a positive-stop foot change, with a one down, three up change pattern — that is press the lever down for first gear, then up for neutral, second, third and fourth. The clutch was operated by a long vertical arm along the middle of the case, with the cable sitting in an abutment on the top of the case, making cable changes relatively easy. The clutch adjuster was accessible through a circular screw-in alloy cover between the gear lever and kick-starter pedals. The outer casing on the timing side housed the clutch and gear change operating mechanisms, and the inner cover carried the main and lay shaft on ball bearings. A gear indicator was mounted on the front of the box, with a pointer driven from the gear change quadrant. The pointer registered against a brass scale on the top of the box, which was calibrated with 1, N, 2, 3 and 4, giving the rider an indication of which gear was engaged.

Internally the gearbox was typical of the designs used in the majority of British bikes at the time. It comprised a main shaft and lay shaft, with four gear pinions on each and a pinion sliding on each shaft to give the four gear ratios. The input and output shafts were concentric, with the clutch driving the main shaft and with the output sprocket splined onto the concentric top gear pinion and sitting behind the clutch and primary chain case. The sliding pinions were moved by a pair of selector forks that were operated by a rotating camplate driven from the gear change pedal. The box pivoted about its bottom mount to adjust the primary chain tension and received a good reception from the press.

The standard Triumph four-speed gearbox was a strong and robust unit.

The 1950+ gearbox was redesigned to cope with the 650cc units. Both pre- and post-1950 Triumph gearboxes had a gear indicator mounted on the upper front of the unit. A brass strip and pointer shows which gear is engaged.

The primary drive was fully enclosed in an attractive two-piece alloy oil bath — many of Triumph's rivals were still using pressed steel cases. The front footrest was bolted through the case, helping to locate it, and there were twelve screws around the periphery of the outer case giving a good chance of keeping the oil inside where it belonged. The outer case had a large streamlined bulge to cover the engine shock absorber and the whole case was polished. Inside the case a single-row chain took the drive from the engine sprocket to the four-spring multi-plate clutch, which had four drive plates with cork inserts (three on the 3T) and four plain driven plates. The clutch was operated by a push rod that ran through the gearbox main shaft and was connected to the clutch operating mechanism in the gearbox outer cover on the timing side.

The first major change to the gearbox came in 1948, when the introduction of the sprung hub meant that there was no provision for a speedometer drive on the rear wheel, so it was moved to be driven from the back of the gearbox casing. Initially fitted only to machines fitted with the sprung hub, from 1949 all models had this modification.

For 1950 the gearbox was completely redesigned to enable it to cope with the additional power produced by the 650cc Thunderbird. The redesign resulted in completely new shafts and gears, which were not interchangeable with earlier boxes, and included a proper garter seal on the output shaft bearing on the machined shoulder of the final drive sprocket, in an effort to keep the gearbox oil in the case. The speedometer drive was repositioned in the leading edge of the right hand side inner cover, where a right angle drive was driven off a gear on the lay shaft, and the cable bolted onto the front of the inner cover. The introduction of the swinging arm frame in 1954 saw changes to the gearbox casing, but the internals remained unchanged.

The Triumph gearbox was fitted with the Slickshift mechanism for 1958. This meant that the clutch operating lever was changed from a vertical to a horizontal alignment.

The Slickshift Gearbox

Apart from some minor internal changes over the years, the next big change was the introduction of the Slickshift gearbox for 1958. Fitted to all the big Pre-unit twins in the range for 1958, this feature integrated the gearshift and the clutch operating mechanisms. When the gear lever was pushed it also lifted the clutch, so the rider did not have to use the hand lever. The mechanism worked, and some American dirt track racers used it to considerable effect on fast starts, since they could push the gearlever down to select first gear and, by just keeping their foot on the gear lever, they kept the clutch disengaged and only had to let their foot off the lever when the flag went down. However, it was not popular with sporting riders in the UK and was often disconnected. An easy recognition feature for the Slickshift box was that the clutch operating lever was now horizontal on the top of the gearbox, operating the clutch push rod via an internal vertical shaft, and the clutch adjuster cover was now oval and held on with two screws. When it was introduced in 1959, the Bonneville was not equipped with the Slickshift – a tacit admission by the factory that the mechanism was not suitable for a sports model. Slickshift was dropped for 1962, with the cryptic statement from the factory that it had 'outlived its usefulness'. The following year saw the introduction of the 'B' Series Unit twins and the end of the Pre-unit range, apart from the production of a few more batches of TRWs to meet outstanding orders.

The primary drive fitted to the Pre-unit models was conventional: an engine sprocket with a sprung-loaded shock absorber drove a single-row chain to a multi-plate clutch – in the Triumph's case a four-spring unit with multiple friction and plain plates. The whole drive was encased in a light alloy chain case, with the outer cover retained by screws around its periphery. This design was much less prone to leakage than rival units, many of which used pressed steel cases and single central screw fixings. The outer case carried a large styled bulge to cover the engine shock absorber.

With the introduction of the alternator electrics the design of the outer case was changed, initially to carry a circular steel cover for the alternator when it was mounted in the outer case. When the alternator was mounted on studs onto the inner case, the outer cover lost the steel cover and some models had the model name cast into the outer cover. The case used on the swinging-arm framed bikes was shorter than that on the rigid framed models.

The pre-alternator Triumphs had a spring-loaded engine shock absorber on the end of the crankshaft. The primary chain case had a streamlined bulge to accommodate it.

The primary chain was a single-row affair on all Pre-unit Triumphs. Note the crankshaft shock absorber on this Tiger 100.

The first alternators were mounted in a redesigned outer primary chain case. A chromed cover on the case allowed the alignment of the alternator to be measured. The transmission shock absorber was fitted in the clutch.

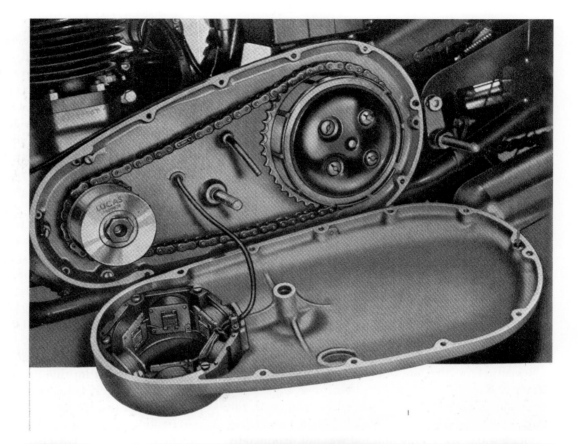

The later alternator-equipped engines had the stator mounted on the inner chain case. The outer case lost the chrome cover.

Frame

Rigid and Sprung Hub

When the Speed Twin was introduced to the public at the end of 1937, it displayed Turner's ability to make use of what already existed by using a lightly modified frame and running gear from the singles range. This frame was typical of the time and of brazed lug construction. This is where the main elements of the frame, such as the steering head, engine mounts, wheel mounts and joining lugs, are formed from cast iron and joined by pinning and brazing together straight steel tubes. This provides a rigid, strong structure, but tends to be weighty. The practice came directly from the pedal cycle industry and was adapted to the needs of the motor cycle industry at the start of the 20th century. It was a good economical method at the time and made the production of frames without specialist skills or jigs easy.

Nevertheless, this method of frame building was slowly replaced by welding pre-bent tubes together, a technique adopted in the 1950s by Norton, with the Featherbed, and BSA, with the A7/A10 swinging arm frame, but the brazed lug method was not dropped by Triumph until the early 1970s with the Umberslade-designed frame. Even then, the 500cc twin persisted with its brazed lug frame until it was replaced by the frame derived from the BSA B50 in the TR5T Adventurer/Trophy Trail during 1974.

The Speed Twin frame was made in two sections. The front comprised the headstock, which had a pair of tubes forming the top rail – a large diameter tube on top and a smaller diameter example below to triangulate the steering head. The front down tube was also brazed into the headstock and had lugs on it to mate with the front engine plates and the rear section engine rails. The top-rail tubes were brazed into a front lug, which also carried the seat tube, running downwards. This tube had a lug to locate the gearbox adjuster and rear engine plates, and a second lug at the bottom to mate to the lower rails of the rear frame section. The rear section comprised two straight tubes running from the top of the seat tube lug to the rear wheel and a second pair of tubes running from the rear wheel under the engine and gearbox, which were bolted into the bottom lug of the seat tube and the bottom lug of the front down tube. This pair of tubes was braced with a cross tube top and bottom, just in front of the rear wheel. The bottom of the gearbox was located on a single stud that spanned the bottom rails, and it pivoted around this stud. A top bracket was bolted to the top of the gearbox and had an adjusting slot that was clamped to the seat tube lug to allow the gearbox the movement needed primary drive chain adjustment. The frame had no provision for rear wheel suspension and until the introduction of the swinging arm frames in 1954, the only rear wheel suspension offered by Triumph was its patented sprung hub, which fitted the rigid frame with no modifications.

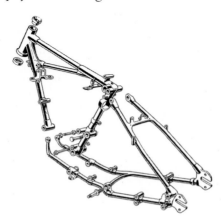

The original rigid Triumph twin frame was of cast lug and brazed tube construction. The rear half bolted to the bottom of the front down tube, and the top and bottom of the seat tube.

The TR5 frame was similar to the 3T frame and identical to the TRW frame. Slightly shorter than the 5T and Tiger 100 unit, the front down tube was connected to the rear section using a pair of engine plates.

When it was introduced in 1939, the Tiger 100 frame was subtly different from that of the Speed Twin, with a slightly changed steering head angle to give more trail and improve handling. The Speed Twin inherited this frame for the 1940 model year.

For 1951 the 6T and Speed Twin retained the previous year's frame, but the Tiger 100's frame received subtle changes. The engine gained a front head steady, which required a new bracket on the front down tube, and the rear section received stronger rear wheel abutments.

The same rigid frame layout as seen on the Speed Twin and Tiger 100 was used for the 3T but was a lighter build and slightly shorter than that used on the 500cc twins. A useful distinguishing point between the two frames is that the 3T front frame section has a brazed-on lug for the front fuel tank mount on the lower top rail and the rear fuel tank mount is incorporated into the rear lug, while the 500cc frame has separate bolt-on lugs.

The rigid TR5 Trophy frame followed the general layout of the 3T and 5T frames, but differed in detail. As an on/off-road bike, the TR5 needed greater ground clearance, while a shorter wheelbase was found to be desirable for off-road action. The TR5 Trophy frame was derived from the 3T frame, but the front down tube was shortened to terminate just above the front-mounted dynamo and had two horizontal tubes fixed through it, one above the other. A long stud passed through each tube and the front engine plates were bolted to these studs. The lower ends of the plates were then bolted to the lower frame rails. This allowed the engine to be mounted slightly further forward than on the other twins, which assisted in reducing wheelbase. The rear engine plates also positioned the engine forwards a little, again to help reduce wheelbase. The gearbox was mounted in the same way as on the other twins, pivoting on its bottom mount to give adjustment to the primary chain. The TR5 fuel tank had two flanges on its front that bolted directly into threaded holes on each side of the steering head lug, and the rear mount of the tank was bolted onto a cast-in lug on the seat tube lug, as on the 3T.

The TRW frame followed the TR5 design and used identical front and rear frame sections to the TR5 from the 1952 model year on. Despite being produced into the mid-1960s, the TRW only used the rigid frame, apart from one swinging arm framed prototype.

The rigid frame of this pre-war Speed Twin is equipped with girder front forks.

The TR5 Trophy was very similar to the road bikes, but with a shorter wheel base.

131

Triumph's first swinging arm frame was a good attempt. However, its handing was not as good as the Norton Featherbed.

The single down tube frame brought the looks of the Tiger 100 up to date.

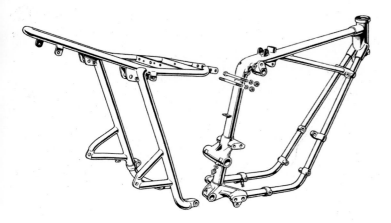

The new-for-1960 duplex front down tube frame was only used on the 650cc bikes. While it was more rigid than the simplex version, it still does not have a reputation for good handling.

Swinging Arm

The Triumph Pre-unit twins were equipped with two models of swinging arm frame, the first appearing in 1954 with a single front down tube (now referred to as the simplex type) and the second appearing in 1960 with twin (duplex) down tubes.

The need to replace the sprung hub with a more versatile method of rear suspension led to Triumph introducing a new swinging arm frame for 1954. In something of a break from the Triumph tradition of introducing major changes to the 'cooking' bikes in its range, the new frame equipped the Tiger 100 and Tiger 110. This policy break was probably due to the increasing level of concern about the handling and road holding of the larger and faster twins, along with demands for more comfort than the sprung hub could deliver. The introduction of the swinging arm frame was probably also due to competition from Triumph's rivals. The Royal Enfield twin had had a swinging arm frame from its introduction in early 1948, as did the AJS/Matchless twins, also from 1948, and Norton's Dominator Deluxe had the superlative Featherbed frame in 1952. However, BSA, probably Triumph's biggest rival at the time, only introduced its swinging arm frame in the same year as the Triumph unit and, of course, BSA had owned Triumph since Sangster's 1951 sale.

The new frame retained the brazed lug construction of the rigid frame and like the rigid frame was made in two halves – a front 'n' shaped unit that carried the steering head and the rear swing arm pivot, and a rear/lower unit that comprised the engine rails and top rear suspension and seat mounts. The front section comprised a large steering head lug and a front down tube that had a pair of lugs to accept the front engine plates. There was a pair of top tubes, a large diameter tube running from the top of the steering head to the seat-post cast lug, and a secondary smaller diameter tube running from the bottom of the steering head lug to the seat post, triangulating the steering head. There was a single rear tube running vertically down from the seat-post lug which carried a lug for the swinging arm pivot and carried on down to an upside down 'T' piece. For the first year of production the frame did not have sidecar lugs fitted. These only appeared for the 1955 season, when the Speed Twin, Thunderbird and Trophy adopted the swinging arm frame.

The bolt-on rear section was of welded construction and comprised a pair of engine/gearbox rails running parallel to the ground, bolted onto the front down tube lower lug and the seat post 'T' piece. These rails then swooped up to be welded to a bracket that carried the shock absorber top mount. A second pair of tubes, with a welded-in bracing tube between them, ran forwards from the shock absorber mount to be bolted in place on the seat-post lug. The swinging arm itself was a one-piece fabricated unit, with tubular arms and a reinforced pivot area. The frame was heavily made and described by Triumph as: 'A simple yet immensely strong design providing magnificent steering and road holding even under the worst possible road or cross country conditions.'

However, this description does not really ring true with contemporary reports or anecdotal evidence today. Contemporary road tests approved of the frame, but reading between the lines the steering was described as light and the steering damper was required at higher speeds – indicating that high-speed

stability was not as good as it should have been. This manifest itself as the infamous Triumph weave, which appeared during high-speed cornering and seems to have been caused by the somewhat spindly swinging arm, the absence of any significant reinforcement around the swinging arm mounts, and the slim and flexible front forks. Turner refused to believe that there was anything wrong with either the geometry or the handling of the frame, despite reports from his development team and the testers, so little could be done to rectify the problem. The bolt-up design of the frame was never going to be as rigid as its BSA or Norton all-welded rivals and the lack of bracing on the swinging arm pivot was always going to lead to problems, especially when there was some wear in the swinging arm bushes. During the 1960s and 1970s, early swinging arm Triumphs gain a probably exaggerated reputation for bad handling, no doubt aided and assisted by worn out cycle parts, and this probably contributed to the 1960s' specials market activity of plonking the easily-tuned Triumph engines into Nor-

The duplex-framed Bonneville was a good bike, but not among the best for handling.

ton, BSA and all sorts of other frames. However, despite the anecdotal evidence, probably the most telling evidence of shortcomings in this frame design was twofold: the replacement of the single down tube frame with the duplex unit in 1960, and the appearance of major bracing on the 500cc and 650cc twins swinging arm pivots in the 1960s. These modifications to the Unit Triumph's frames at last provided handling that matched their performance and were due to the efforts of Doug Hele and Bert Hopwood, but were only possible once Turner had retired.

So the new swinging arm frame was not ideal, but it spread to the other twins in the range, the 5T Speed Twin, TR5 Trophy and 6T Thunderbird for 1956, and remained broadly the same with only minor modifications until it was replaced for the 1960 season.

The new frame for 1960 had one major change from the previous year's item – the single front down tube was replaced with two down tubes, giving the frame its 'Duplex' name. It has been speculated that the frame only had twin down tubes to mimic the twin down tube BSA and Norton twin frames, both of which handled better than the Triumph twin. However, Triumph did not take the opportunity to provide better support for its swinging arm or uprate its front forks, so the slightly unsettling Triumph weave persisted.

The new frame had a major fault, which only showed up when the bikes were hammered in off-road events in the USA. The front down tubes could fracture just below the steering head and this led to fatalities in racing, one of which was witnessed by Turner in the December 1960 Big Bear race in California. An immediate rectification programme resulted in the frame gaining a second top rail that ran horizontally from the top of the down tubes back to the top rail during the 1960 model year. This triangulated the steering head and cured the fracturing problem. At the same time the steering head angle was altered from 67 degrees to 65 degrees to improve steering. The new frame was stronger, but the vibration damping characteristics had been changed by the improvement and resulted in a spate of fuel tank strap breakages and increased vibration felt by the rider. The problem was solved by a redesign of the tank fixing and the frame continued in the revised form for the 1961 and 1962 model years with minimal changes.

Suspension

In line with most British motor cycles, the Speed Twin featured girder forks when it was introduced. These were similar to those used on the singles in the range and comprised a one-piece girder assembly, made from steel tube, which carried the front wheel and mudguard. The girder was joined to the steering head by a set of four links and the links allowed for upwards and downwards movement by acting as a parallelogram. A spring was mounted between the steering head and the girder assembly, and friction dampers were mounted on the lower pair of links. Initially the Speed Twin used longer lower links, approximately 45/32in (105mm) long, while the 1939 Tiger 100 girder forks had different lower links approximately 315/16in (100mm) long to compensate for the differing head angle and to preserve the 54in wheelbase with the new Tiger 100 frame. These were standardised for the Speed Twin and Tiger 100 when the Speed Twin gained the Tiger 100 frame for 1940. At the same time the forks saw the addition of check springs between the top and bottom links to improve wheel control. While girder forks were rigid and gave good wheel control, they offered limited wheel movement, friction damping and high unsprung weight. During the war, Triumph therefore looked closely at the use of telescopic forks, as seen on the German BMWs and Matchless WD singles; when production restarted in 1946, Triumph offered its own take on the telescopic fork. Its forks comprised a set of yokes (or triple trees) running on cup and cone bearings in the steering head. Each stanchion was clamped in the yokes and fitted into a lower, steel, fork leg. Two bushes, one fixed at the top of the slider and one on the bottom of the stanchion, allowed the bottom leg to slide up and down on the stanchion. The wheel was fixed to the bottom of the fork leg by a push-in spindle, locked in position by a pinch bolt on the drive side leg and a nut on the spindle. The forks had internal springs, held in place by the stanchion top nuts. A tapered damper rod was bolted into the bottom of the fork leg and an oil damper rod fitted to the stanchion was used to progressively restrict oil flow, giving one way damping. The exposed surfaces of the forks were initially covered with long tubular steel covers with headlamp 'ears', but with the advent of the nacelle for 1949

Pre-war the Tiger 100 and Speed Twin were equipped with girder forks.

Post-war Triumphs had telescopic front forks with internal springs. This nacelle-equipped Speed Twin is typical.

The Trophy models kept the sporting separate headlamp and speedometer also seen on the early post-war Speed Twin and Tiger 100.

The nacelle had only been fitted to the touring bikes in the range by 1960. The TR6 (seen here) and the Bonneville both had separate headlamps.

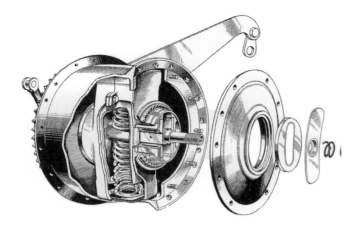

Rear suspension was delivered at minimal cost by the bolt-on sprung hub, introduced in 1946.

The sprung hub was a neat and unobtrusive way of giving a couple of inches of rear wheel movement. It is seen here on a Thunderbird.

The inner spring carrier of the sprung hub had a cast-in warning notice. The springs inside were under a great deal of compression.

these were replaced with a pair of nacelle bottom covers. The Trophy retained the long covers until the introduction of rubber bellows to cover the stanchions in 1955. The forks gained new legs with a clamp-on front wheel for 1957. The T120 Bonneville joined the TR6 Trophy, with a separate headlamp and rubber gaiters over the stanchions in 1960.

In general the Triumph telescopic fork was good, but it was not as rigid as offerings from BSA and Norton, and prone to flexing. The steel lower fork legs were heavier than the Norton 'Roadholder' units and made an unwelcome contribution to the unsprung weight of the suspension, while the one way damping was not state of the art by the 1960s.

The Spring Wheel, as Triumph called it, was probably better known as the sprung hub. It was Triumph's first attempt to provide rear suspension and offered as an extra across the range from September 1946 for the 1947 model year. The unit was a bolt on affair and comprised, as the name implies, a complete rear hub with built in suspension. The axle was fixed to a square guide assembly that carried three springs – below the axle were inner and outer main springs and above it was a rebound spring. The axle guide and springs were placed in a two-part bolt-up cast alloy 'plunger guide box' where it could move up and down in an arc to maintain rear chain tension. The rest of the hub, along with a substantial 8in diameter brake, was built onto the plunger guide box and the wheel rim was fixed to the hub using short, straight pull spokes. The wheel revolved on large diameter bearings that had to accommodate the axle movement of a couple of inches within their inner races. When the axle was bolted into the frame the whole wheel could move up and down against the springs, giving limited rear wheel movement. Triumph claimed 2in of movement, which was comparable to their rivals' plunger units and certainly better than nothing. In addition, the system kept chain tension constant, giving he chain an easier life than some plunger devices. The friction of the parts provided some damping, but the unit was not particularly sophisticated in that respect. The complete assembly weighed approximately 17lb (7.71kg) more than a conventional rear wheel. Due to some failures in service, probably due to misadjustment, the bearings in the sprung hub were uprated in 1950 from cup and cone to 3½in (89mm) diameter journal ball races, which were non-adjustable. From then on, rear wheel bearing failures became very rare since the bearings were so large they rarely wore out. One feature of the sprung hub was the cast-in warning on the plunger guide box: 'WARNING – Disassemble only with special tool'. Care was needed because of the three springs trapped under considerable tension in the box.

The sprung hub was superseded by the swinging arm frame in 1954, equipping the road sports Tiger 100 and 110. The swinging arm was a one-piece fork that pivoted on bushes on a steel pin located in a cast lug on the seat tube of the new frame. The arm's up and down movement was controlled by Girling shock absorbers, with shrouds covering the springs. This basic design was carried forwards to the duplex frame introduced in 1960.

Girder-forked machines had a 7in front brake with built-in speedometer drive.

Wheels and Brakes

The 1938 Speed Twin was fitted with a 19in diameter rear wheel and a 20in diameter front, both of WM2 width. The front and rear hubs were half-width items and carried 7in diameter by 1⅛ inch width single leading shoe brakes. The front brake featured an alloy back plate and a forward facing brake lever, and a speedometer drive was incorporated on the brake plate and driven from a gear inside the brake drum. A flat steel torque arm was mounted on the front on the brake plate and fixed to the front fork. This brake continued through to 1940.

With the return of peace and the introduction of Triumph's telescopic front fork, a 19in front wheel and a new design of front brake was fitted to the Speed Twin and Tiger 100 for 1946. It was still a 7in diameter, half-width hub unit with an alloy back plate, but the torque arm was incorporated into and cast with the brake plate and bolted to the rear of the forks. The speedometer drive was now fitted to the rear wheel, but moved to the gearbox for 1948 with the introduction of the sprung hub. The rear wheel was a 19in diameter rim with a half-width hub and a 7in single leading shoe brake. The rear wheel remained a 19in unit for the rest of the model range's production life. The rear brake also remained a 7in diameter unit, except on bikes equipped with the sprung hub, which had an 8in diameter brake.

The pre-war front hub was complex, since it incorporated the speedometer drive. Note the ribbed drum for better cooling.

The early post-war telescopic-forked bikes had a simplified front brake, with a polished alloy back plate.

For 1954 the Tiger 100 and Tiger 110 models took the 'pie crust' half-width 8in front brake with air scoops.

From 1955 the half-width hub lost the crenulations that had given it the 'pie crust' nickname. The big front air scoop looked good and helped to cool the brake.

The full-width front hub appeared in 1958 with a plain front brake.

Aftermarket suppliers provided upgrades for Triumph brakes. Here is a 1960 twin leading shoe conversion.

ABOVE: *Apart from the sprung hub 8in unit, all the Triumph Pre-unit twins were equipped with 7in diameter rear brakes. All were rod operated. This is a 1938 Speed Twin unit.*

TOP RIGHT: *With the change to swinging arm frame in the mid 1950s, the rear brake remained as a 7 inch diameter single leading shoe rod operated unit.*

RIGHT: *This TR5 Trophy is equipped with the quickly detachable rear wheel – an option across the range of swinging arm-framed Triumphs.*

Triumph introduced its famous Quickly Detachable (QD) rear wheel in 1954, for the Tiger 100 and Tiger 110 equipped with the new swinging arm frame. The wheel was in two parts, with the brake drum and integral rear drive sprocket bolted onto the drive side of the swinging arm using a stub axle. The wheel mated to the drum with a spline. Removal of the wheel spindle and a spacer from the timing side allowed the wheel to be pulled off the spline and removed without disturbing the drive chain or rear brake. This feature was offered as an extra on the entire range of swinging arm Pre-unit Triumphs.

In 1954 Triumph introduced a new 8in single leading shoe front brake, along with a new half width hub. The hub was nicknamed the 'pie crust' since it had indentations around the spoke flange, and the alloy brake plate featured a large air scoop on its front and an extractor scoop on its rear to aid cooling. Fitted to the Tiger 100 and Tiger 110, the brake was a signifi-

cantly better unit than the 7in item fitted to the rest of the range. The hub design was changed to remove the pie crust crenulations for 1955, since they had been prone to cracking, but the rest of the brake remained unchanged. The TR6 Trophy model was also fitted with this brake for its second year of production in 1957.

In 1958, Triumph introduced new full width front hubs and new front brakes across the range. The Tiger 100, Tiger 110 and Trophy TR6 got an 8in diameter brake, while the 5T, 6T and Trophy had a 7in diameter unit. Both the new 7 and 8in diameter brakes were single leading shoe units with plain alloy back plates and no air scoops. The 7in brake and hub was retained only on the 6T Thunderbird for 1959, while the Trophy, T100, T110 and T120 all got the 8in full width hub brake. For the remaining years of production, all the Pre-unit bikes were fitted with the 8in front brake in the full width hub.

All pre-nacelle Speed Twins and Tiger 100s had an instrument panel in the top of the fuel tank. It included an inspection light, oil pressure gauge, ammeter and light switch.

The Triumph streamlined nacelle carried the speedometer, ammeter, engine kill button and light switch. Produced in a number of designs, coil ignition bikes had a combined lights and ignition switch.

The off road TR5 (and TR6) never had the nacelle fitted. Here an early TR5 shows its separate speedometer and tank rack.

Instrumentation and Controls

From the introduction of the Speed Twin through to 1949 and the introduction of the nacelle, all the Triumph twins were fitted with an instrument panel on the fuel tank. This was diamond shaped and made from black Bakelite with a textured fitting. It carried the 0–100psi oil pressure gauge, light switch, inspection light and ammeter. The whole panel sat on a pre-formed rubber pad to protect the tank paintwork and provide limited protection from the vertical twin's vibration.

For 1939 the oil pressure gauge was changed for a unit that read up to 160psi. The inspection light was wired such that it came on with the lights and the panel was arranged so that the inspection light illuminated the ammeter and oil pressure gauge. This was changed back to the original 1938 light for the 1940 models due to complaints about dazzle. The Bakelite panel was replaced from 1940 with a steel version, as previously used on the singles, since the Bakelite unit was prone to cracking. The steel unit sat on a rubber bead and was fixed in place with a single screw in its centre. It was painted using crinkle-finish matt black paint. The oil pressure gauge was changed back to a 100psi-reading unit for 1946. The tank top panel remained unchanged until 1949, when the nacelle was introduced. The ammeter and light switch were relocated to the nacelle top, but the inspection light was deleted and the oil pressure gauge was replaced by a pop out indicator in the timing case.

The 1938 Speed Twin was fitted with a 3½in diameter 120mph Smiths chronometric speedometer. Mounted on a bracket at the top of the front forks, it took its drive by cable from a gearbox fixed to the front brake back plate.

On the launch of the Tiger 100 for the 1939 model year, Triumph also introduced the renowned Triumph 'Rev-o-lator' speedometer, which was also fitted to the Speed Twin. This 3½in diameter Smiths chronometric instrument had three bands on its face giving the engine revs for a given speed in second, third and top gears. Really of limited use, it was another example of Turner's design flair, giving a rev counter to the rider without the cost of having to have a separate instrument and the associated drive.

With the introduction of the nacelle in 1949, the ammeter and light switch migrated to the nacelle and the oil pressure gauge and inspection light were deleted. The Rev-o-lator 120mph speedometer was placed in the centre of the top of the nacelle, along with the kill button.

Handlebars

All of the Pre-unit Triumphs, with the exception of the Trophy models, used 1in diameter handlebars with the throttle end swaged down to enable the fitment of a 7/8in twist grip. The standard Triumph twist grip used for most of the Pre-unit twins featured a knurled brass thumbscrew that controlled a friction damper. This could be adjusted to stiffen up the throttle action, giving a crude 'cruise control' to the rider. For 1946 the headlamp dip/main was handled by a round, chromed, pressed steel Lucas flick switch (type 380,057) that clamped on the handlebars. The horn press and magneto cut-out buttons also clamped onto the handlebars and were identical Lucas units (type 762,080). With the introduction of the nacelle in 1949, the handlebar layout was tidied up with a new horn button that bolted through the handlebars on the clutch side, its wires concealed in the bars, and a new dip switch mounted on the back of the brake lever clamp. This arrangement of handlebar-mounted switches continued on all bikes fitted with the nacelle.

The nacelle was never fitted to any of the Trophy models. The 500cc and later 650 Trophy models had their speedometer (and, when fitted, tachometer) mounted on a bracket fixed to the top yoke, and had a separate headlamp with ammeter and light switch fitted in the rear of the headlamp shell. This lasted until 1960, when the light switch (Lucas type 88 SA) was moved to the right hand side of the machine under the nose of the seat, as on the Bonneville. Handlebar switches comprised a dip switch, horn button and cut-out button, all of which clamped onto the 7/8in handlebars.

A tachometer was not standard on any Triumph (apart from the GP) until the introduction of a tachometer driven from a gearbox housed in a modified timing cover for the 1960 US market TR6/A and TR7/A roadster models. This was not listed in the brochures at the time. The tachometer was a Smiths 3½in diameter chronometric unit that matched the

speedometer and both were mounted on a neat steel bracket bolted to the fork top yoke. At this time the speedometer on the 1960-on TR6 and T120 was changed for a 140mph unit to reflect the sports models' increased performance. US distributors offered tachometer kits from the late 1950s, with the drive taken from the end of the exhaust camshaft via a gearbox in a modified timing cover. Various brackets were supplied to fit the tachometer to the handlebars of machines fitted with the nacelle.

The 1960 Bonneville and TR6s could be supplied with a tachometer as a factory option. The drive was taken from the timing cover and the instrument was mounted on the top fork yoke, alongside the speedometer, giving the classic sports look.

A late TR6 shows a similar layout to the early TR5.

Electrics

The Speed Twin electrics were state of the art for the day. The sparks for the ignition and 6-volt DC power for the lights and battery were supplied by a Lucas Magdyno. The Magdyno was a common fitting at the time and comprised a magneto with a dynamo mounted on top of it, driven from the Magdyno drive gear and making up a combined unit that could be driven from a single source. In the Speed Twin's case the drive source was the exhaust camshaft pinion, which meshed with the Magdyno gear to drive the magneto armature and, through this gear, a second gear to drive the dynamo. The unit was equipped with a manual advance and retard mechanism for the ignition timing and the dynamo was an E3HMLO unit pushing out 40 watts.

The Speed Twin had an 8in diameter chromed head-lamp and the 6-volt battery was mounted on a platform on the drive side, retained by a steel strap. The Tiger 100 followed this specification when it was introduced in 1939. Post-war, the Lucas Magdyno was replaced by a separate magneto and 6-volt dynamo. The magneto was a BT-H unit with automatic advance and retard, mounted in the same spot behind the barrels as the Magdyno and was driven from the inlet camshaft pinion. The separate Lucas dynamo was mounted on the front of the engine, with its drive taken from the exhaust camshaft pinion.

The 3T De-luxe electrical system was similar to that of the Speed Twin, with a separate magneto and dynamo mounted in the Speed Twin positions, but the magneto could be a BT-H or Lucas unit and was

The pre-war Speed Twin was equipped with a magdyno, a combined magneto and dynamo mounted behind the barrels.

equipped with advance retard. In all other respects the 6-volt system mirrored that of the Speed Twin.

The first major change to the electrical system came with the introduction of an alternator system to provide AC power. This required the use of a solid state rectifier to convert the AC output of the alternator to DC and current regulation was achieved by switching in more alternator coils as the demand for current increased; when the lights were turned on for example. The system was first introduced on the 1953 Speed Twin when the magneto and dynamo were deleted and a coil ignition system installed. The alternator was mounted on the drive side, with a magnetic rotor mounted on the end of the crank and a six-coil stator mounted on the inside of the primary chain case cover. At a stroke this removed the need for a separate

dynamo drive and provided more power from a much cheaper and more reliable package. In the case of the Speed Twin and Thunderbird, the components needed to provide coil ignition were a lot cheaper than a magneto. The contact breaker points were mounted in a distributor in place of the magneto and the coil was mounted somewhat inelegantly on top of the distributor. The system was also fitted to the Thunderbird for 1954. The Tiger 100 retained the magneto and dynamo through to its replacement with the Unit Construction T100A at the end of 1959. The other bikes in the range gained the alternator to generate current to charge the battery for lighting in 1960, but retained the magneto to provide the sparks until their replacement with the new Unit Construction models for the 1963 model year.

Post-war the dynamo was moved to the front of the engine and the magneto remained behind the barrels.

The coil-ignition twins had a distributor mounted in the old magneto position, driven from the inlet camshaft, with the coil mounted on top. This is a 6T Thunderbird.

Performance Figures

The Triumph Pre-unit Twin range spanned some four decades, from the 1930s through to the 1960s, and the models were continuously developed to provide increases in performance, refinement and reliability, with new models introduced at regular intervals. The following tables take contemporary road test data for various models.

Speed Twin, 1937–1953

Source and date	Top Speed	0-60 mph/seconds	Braking distance from 30mph	Fuel consumption
The Motor Cycle, 21 October 1937	93.75 mph (150km/h)	Not tested	30ft (9.14m) 29ft (8.83m)	82.2mpg (3.44ltr/100km) at 40mph (64km/h)
Motor Cycling, 17 January 1946	90 mph (144km/h)	9.5		66mpg (4.29ltr/100km) (town)
Motor Cycling, 17 March 1949	88 mph (141km/h)	9	30ft (9.14m)	77mpg (3.68ltr/100km) (country)
Motor Cycling, 13 August 1953	91 mph (146km/h)	10	32ft (9.75m)	67mpg (4.22ltr/100km) (town) 74mpg (3.82ltr/100km) (country) 62mpg (4.56ltr/100km) at 50 mph (80km/h)

Tiger 100, 1937–1953

Source and date	Top Speed	Standing start ¼ mile/seconds	Braking distance from 30mph	Fuel consumption
The Motor Cycle, 16 November 1939	98mph (157km/h)	16.5 16.8	28ft (8.53m) 25ft (7.62m)	57mpg (4.96ltr/100km) (town) 63mpg (4.49ltr/100km) (country)
The Motor Cycle, 14 April 1949	93mph (150km/h)			66mpg (4.29ltr/100km) (town) 77mpg (3.68ltr/100km) (country)

650cc Models

Model	Source and date	Top Speed	Standing start ¼ mile/seconds	Braking distance from 30mph	Fuel consumption
1951 Thunderbird	*Motor Cycling*, 30 November 1950	100mph (160km/h) 101mph (163km/h) (highest one way recorded at 109mph/175km/h)	16	30ft (9.14m)	72mpg (3.93ltr/100km) at 50mph (80km/h)
1956 Tiger 110	*The Motor Cycle*, 8 March 1956		16	33ft (10.06m)	80mpg (3.54ltr/100km) at 50mph (80km/h)
1961 Trophy	*The Motor Cycle*, 15 June 1961	101mph (163km/h) (highest one way recorded at 105mph/169km/h)	15.1	30ft 6in (9.30m)	81mpg (3.49ltr/100km) at 50mph (80km/h)
1962 Bonneville	*Cycle World*, January 1962	108mph (174km/h) (highest one way recorded at 110mph/177km/h)	14.5	Not Tested	Between 40 and 70mpg (7.08 and 4.04ltr/100km)

As can be seen from these figures, the performance of the Triumph twin improved over the years, but usually in relatively small steps. Over time, while the engine outputs increased, so did the sophistication of the machines, resulting in increased weight that counteracted the greater power. So while a Tiger 100 was truthfully named and would 'top the ton', only a very good, well set up Tiger 110 would reach 110mph, and 105mph was more common. Surprisingly, contemporary road tests show the T120 Bonneville would usually make about 110' and only with special tuning would it approach 120mph, with *Motor Cycling* getting 117mph from a factory tuned machine.

Triton – Rockers' Revenge

The Triton was the ultimate expression of the motor cycle cafe racer and rocker culture of the late 1950s and 1960s, and is still a powerful icon today. Conventional thought is that the Triton merges the strongest elements of two of the main players in the British motor cycle industry of the 1950 and 1960s: Norton's superb handling Featherbed frame, and Triumph's flexible, reliable, tunable and cheap twin engine. It is fairly certain that no one made a Nor-umph, a Norton engine in a Triumph frame, since this would give the worst of both worlds, a poor handling bike with an expensive and unreliable engine!

Initially the main driver behind the evolution of the Triton was the Formula 500 car racing series that emerged after World War Two and remained popular up to the end of the 1950s. Companies such as Cooper, JBS and Kieft all designed and supplied cars for this class of racing, either as complete units or without engines and gearboxes. The best power units were 500cc singles from Norton and JAP. The latter was in the business of supplying engines and was happy to sell to manufacturers and individuals, but Norton made bikes and the only way to get hold of a new Manx Norton engine and gearbox was to buy a complete Manx Norton. This led to a small supply of Manx Norton rolling chassis being 'available' and the logical engine and gearbox to put into the redundant chassis was the Triumph twin, which was readily available second hand, was a lot cheaper than a Manx engine and was readily tuned. The Triumph-powered Manx Featherbed chassis were initially used by club racers to provide a relatively cheap, good handling ride. John Viccers was an early adopter of the concept, building a number of 'JV Specials' with new Manx Norton frames and Triumph twin engines and gearboxes, which were raced competitively in the 1950s.

It was not long, however before the concept gained ground and began to spawn specials that were road registered, giving riders a replica of the bikes they saw racing on the track. With the Triumph engine providing a dynamo drive (and later an alternator), the bikes could easily be equipped with lights, while the Triumph engine and gearbox, if not too highly tuned, was tractable and reliable and could still give a good turn of speed. As the 1950s progressed the Triton slowly became accepted as a road bike as well as a racing tool, and a cottage industry grew up to supply parts such as engine plates to make the process of slotting the Triumph engine into the Featherbed easier and within the capabilities of the average mechanic.

(continued overleaf)

This is a typical, traditional Triton, with a Bonneville head and tacho drive taken from the timing cover.

Triton – Rockers' Revenge *(continued)*

Rockers and the Cafe Racer

As the 1950s progressed and motorcycling embraced the new youth culture, the Triton became the symbol of the Rockers and the Cafe Racer, and the ultimate expression of the motor cycle culture. As the Manx Norton racers became less competitive, more and more were converted into Tritons, and the ultimate Triton was an ex-Manx rolling chassis with a highly tuned, twin-carburettor Bonnie engine, or even, in the later 1960s, a Bonnie-specification bottom end with a Morgo 750 conversion, Rickman eight-valve head and all the light alloy goodies from the Unity Equipe catalogue. Alongside the ex-racing bikes, the supply of used Featherbed-framed road going Nortons was fairly good by the late 1950s. Often an old and tired Featherbed 500cc ES2 would gain a new lease of life with a Triumph 'heart transplant', or a blown Dominator engine would be replaced with a cheaper and more readily available Triumph twin. Tritons were not necessarily performance 'motors' – there were probably as many 'bog standard' all-iron 6T engines grafted into a 'bog standard' worn out Norton road Featherbed frame, to replace a blown up motor as cheaply as possible, as there were no expense spared, race tuned Cafe Racer beauties.

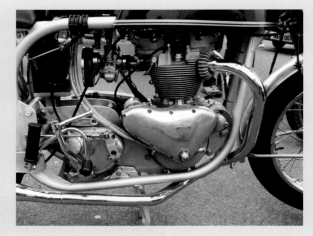

Clockwise from top left:

This Triton has a Bonneville head and a Triumph gearbox. The iron barrel indicates a 650cc engine.

This Triton has a Tiger 100 engine, with its close-finned alloy head, and a Norton gearbox. The bike has the obligatory rear-set footrests.

The drive side of this Tiger 100-engined Triton shows the use of a magneto and dynamo, along with a Triumph primary chain case.

Despite this pragmatic approach to keeping a bike on the road, the Triton still retains a mystique and is one of the few specials that have an intrinsic worth all of their own. The efforts of numerous Triton builders, including Dresda (run by Dave Degans), gave the Triton is own competition history and examples are still being put together in the 2010s. There is a thriving industry making replica Featherbed frames and all the alloy parts a customiser needs to build his or her own interpretation of the Triton theme. A classic Triton can be an expression of the owner's taste and will usually be a Cafe Racer, with clip-ons and rear sets; tuned, twin-carb engine; a large alloy fuel tank; a central oil tank; speedo and tacho on polished alloy brackets; and lots of highly polished alloy accessories. It is a simple formula, echoing the racing bikes of the 1950s and '60s, but with its own style, within which the owner can add individual touches to make the bike unique. The Cafe Racer is arguably the British contribution to the art of customising motor cycles and is deeply rooted in the Rocker culture of the 1960s; the Triton is the ultimate Cafe Racer.

An interesting take on the Triton theme, this is a re-engined Dominator retaining all its Norton tinware and gearbox. The engine is an all-iron 6T Thunderbird unit, making for a lovely touring twin.

The Thunderbird chain case houses an alternator to provide AC electrics, keeping the bike practical.

Customise – Choppers and Bobbers

The Triton was not the only expression of individuality that customisers inflicted on Turner's classic; the Chopper scene that exploded in the early 1970s led to some good, bad and ugly customisations of the basic Triumph twin. Following the motor cycle road movie *Easy Rider*, a large percentage of amateur and professional customisers in the UK based their interpretation of the genre on the ubiquitous British vertical twin, rather than the expensive and rare (in the UK) Harley. Triumphs made up a good proportion of the bikes converted.

The range of custom machines was wide, from lightly bobbed machines to full-dress choppers, with raked frames and massively extended forks. While not to all tastes, the bikes represent an important aspect of the British custom scene and many of the high-quality machines deserve recognition in their own right.

Spotted at a Kempton Park autojumble, this neat bobber is a typical modern day custom Triumph.

The Kempton bobber's engine has an iron barrel and Bonneville twin-carb cylinder head.

The hard-tail frame looks to be a custom made item, although the front frame loop may be standard Triumph. Late Triumph front forks finish off the unraked front end.

This Triumph Thunderbird Chopper was based on a 1951 model and built in 1970 by Reg Sayers from Brighton, UK. It was at the South of England RealClassic Bike Show at Ardingly, in October 2010.

The Thunderbird frame was raked and stretched by 2in (51mm) to give the 'Easy Rider' look.

CHAPTER 4

THE PRE-UNIT TWIN
IN COMPETITION

Introduction

This chapter describes Triumph's most significant competition areas and particularly those that had a direct influence on the development of the Pre-unit engined bikes. Under Turner, Triumph had a pragmatic policy when it came to racing; in the period covered by the Pre-unit models the Triumph factory did not offer any formal support or sponsorship to road race riders – the Triumph policy on racing was to bask in the glory if a privateer won and disown them if they did not! Indeed, Turner never saw the point of competing in the top level of road racing, he saw it as a waste of resources, both in engineering effort and disruption to production.

However, despite this policy, Turner recognised that the factory could and did gain from the publicity of racing success, so immediately after the war, when the Tiger 100 was top of the performance charts, Turner gave tacit support to road racing with the GP model. This was short lived as Norton and AJS started to develop their ohc racers, so Turner looked to where his bikes were still competitive and gave very definite and obvious factory support to the development and riders of the off-road Trophy models that competed in the ISDTs. The Trophy models then went on to become successful production bikes in their own right, fully justifying the investment in competition.

In the USA things were very different, and both East and West Coast distributors acknowledged the 'Win on Sunday, Sell on Monday' philosophy with a wide range of sponsorships and rider support given. The sporting scene in the US was much more off-road orientated than that in Europe, suiting Triumph's range.

The competition effort made by Triumph's US agents was backed up with Meriden-supplied race kits, complete machines and other tuning parts, and locally commissioned engineering developments to provide go-faster parts.

Competition Beginnings

Edward Turner's Triumph twin engine had a long and illustrious competition history. It all started in the winter of 1937. That was when Ivan Benedict Wicksteed and Marius Winslow went to see Turner and requested that he lend them a Speed Twin that they could modify and supercharge to make an attempt on the Class 'C' 500cc flying-start lap record at Brooklands. Turner listened to their pitch, agreed that it was a very logical plan and sent them packing without a machine. Wicksteed and Winslow than bought their own Speed Twin and proceeded to supercharge it.

The Arnott supercharger was mounted above the gearbox and driven by a chain from a crankshaft sprocket mounted outboard of the primary drive, but in this position it meant the frame's seat post had to be cut out, which gave rise to some interesting handling characteristics. An innovative feature was the screw 'jack' positioned between the head and the frame top rail in an attempt to keep the head and barrel in place with the increased compression ratio at higher revs when the supercharger was really working. Earlier runs had resulted in the barrel flange cracking, but this makeshift solution worked. It was adopted by classic racers and is still in use today. The bike, with Wicksteed aboard, gained the record in October 1938

The replica of the Wicksteed Tiger 100-based special is housed in the Brooklands Museum.

at a speed of 118.02mph (189.93km/h). Subsequently, Turner offered the pair factory support for future attempts, including a new Tiger 100 engine with a crankshaft specially adapted to carry the supercharger drive and with this engine, again at Brooklands, Wicksteed managed a 124mph (199.46km/h) run down the Railway Straight. At this point the war intervened and the Brooklands track was closed. It never reopened post-war, giving Triumph the record in perpetuity. Wicksteed continued his association with Triumph, however, riding the 1939 Maudes Trophy bikes at Brooklands before it closed.

A replica of the supercharged Triumph was constructed by Titch and Roger Allen in 1986, using the original machine's handlebars and sundry period Triumph parts. At the time of writing this machine was on display at the Brooklands Museum in Weybridge. Marius Winslow died in a car crash not long after the end of World War Two, but Ivan Wicksteed had a long and rewarding life and died in October 1998.

Road Racing – The Tiger 100 GP

The 1946 Manx Grand Prix was won by a specially modified Triumph Tiger 100 ridden by Irishman Ernie Lyons. The Tiger was prepared by Freddie Clarke, a pre-war racer at Brooklands and head of Triumph's Experimental Department. It sported the soon to be famous alloy head and barrel from the generator unit, complete with cast-in lugs for the cooling shrouds, and the standard Tiger 100 frame and telescopic forks were matched to a sprung hub to give limited rear suspension. Twin carburettors, megaphones and a tuned engine, rear-set footrests and drop handlebars and no lighting equipment, completed the bike's specification. The race was run in atrocious weather conditions and the suspect Triumph handling was not improved when the front down tube fractured just above the front engine mount. While the conditions probably helped the Triumph, it was still an epic ride and a great result for Triumph. It proved that the roadster-based bike could be competitive. With the frame repaired, Lyons went on in the following month, October 1946, to beat all comers, two and four wheeled, at the prestigious Shelsy Walsh hill climb.

For 1947 the factory bike was ridden by David Whitworth. He scored a fourth in the Belgian Grand Prix and a third in the Dutch TT races. The bike formed the basis for the factory-built GP model that, while produced in relatively small numbers (approximately 175 were built between 1948 and 1950), achieved results out of all proportion to the time and effort expended on it. The objective of the GP was to provide a mount for 'the non-professional rider to compete on level terms in all types of long and short circuit racing' (to quote Triumph's

The GP model was based on the Tiger 100 and had some success after World War Two.

publicity material of the time), and the GP was firmly based on the production Tiger 100 to keep costs and disruption to production down. It struggled to compete with the top flight works Grand Prix machines like the Manx Norton or the AJS racers, but it did score some successes.

The first major outing for the GP was the 1948 Isle of Man Senior TT, with six GPs entered, but they all retired. This dismal performance was improved upon in the autumn, when Triumph GPs came first, fourth, fifth, seventh, eleventh and twelfth in the 1948 Manx Grand Prix. The following year GPs came in fifth and sixth in the 1949 Senior TT. The GP continued to be campaigned in subsequent years, but competition was hotting up and the bike was not really competitive as the 1950s

dawned. However, two Manx Grand Prix wins by what was really a tuned-up road bike is an impressive vindication of the soundness of the Triumph design. However, overall it reinforced Turner's negative attitude to racing and development had suffered from his aversion to spending money on sport. The GP was the first and last of the Triumph twins to seriously compete in the top flight of European road racing.

With the demise of the GP, it was left to the privateers to carry the Triumph flag in clubmans' racing, and in this they were helped by the factory with its race kit. The factory also produced limited production runs of the T100C for the home racer market and provided various limited runs of special T100RS road racing machines for the US market.

The RAF generator engine provided the alloy head and barrel.

Ernie Lyons signed this GP in the Sammy Miller Museum. Lyons won the 1946 Manx Grand Prix on a similar machine.

Off Road in Europe – The ISDT

The International Six Days Trial, or ISDT, was probably one of the most important and high profile forms of competition in Europe during the immediate post-war years. The event was truly international, with teams from many European countries competing and it was held throughout the 1940s, 50s and 60s. The event was, in essence, a reliability test for production machines and for each of the six days, competitors had to cover a set route made up of a series of sections which had to be completed in a prescribed time. Bikes went through thorough and extensive scrutinering before the event and all major components were marked to ensure that the bikes were not tampered with during the event.

Riders were allowed no external assistance and had to fix any problems with tools and spares that they carried for the event. Limited time was given for the riders to carry out maintenance and the bikes were parked in a secure parc ferme during the night and outside riding hours, when no access was allowed at all.

The routes were significantly long and riders had to cover between 200 and 300 miles (320 and 482km) each day. Points were deducted from riders and teams failing time checks during the six days, or whose machines failed to start in a set time in the morning, and if a rider failed the timed speed run held on the final day. A range of prizes was awarded, based on both team and individual efforts.

The TR5 Trophy was an on/off-road bike originally designed to compete in the ISDT.

This all-iron engined TR5/T110 hybrid competed in the 1954 ISDT, pre-dating the 1956 TR6. It was ridden to a gold medal by works trials ace Jim Alves.

The ISDT Trophy was awarded to the best performing national team mounted on machines manufactured in the team's home country. The International Vase was awarded to the best performing team of national riders on machines not manufactured by the team members' country. Finally, gold medals were awarded to any rider who lost no points, silver medals went to those who lost between 1 and 25 points, and bronze medals went to those who lost between 26 and 50 points.

The event always generated massive publicity in the weekly motor cycle papers and was avidly followed by the British motor cycling public. The event was a test of rider skill, and machine durability and reliability, and as such was incredibly prestigious to win. Significantly, the riders and factory teams competed for medals as well as first place and a good crop of medals for a manufacturer was almost as good as winning the team event. Virtually all the post-war factories recognised the value of the event and many privateers with tacit factory assistance would also enter. Any sort of win would result in lots of advertising to publicise the result and a team win would result in a major advertising blitz by the successful factory. The event did sell bikes, and in Triumph's case it spawned the range of Trophy bikes, which were true ride-to-work during the week and compete-at-the-weekend bikes.

The first Triumph twin entered into the ISDT was a Speed Twin ridden by Alan Jefferies in the ill-fated event held in late August 1939 at Salzburg, Germany. It had to be ended prematurely with the outbreak of World War Two. Triumph's TR5 was probably the most successful post-war British bike, winning manufacturer's trophies six years running from the late 1940s and gaining numerous individual gold awards for its riders.

Road and Track Racing USA

The Triumph 500cc engine was ideally suited to US oval racing, and road-racing converted T100s and Speed Twins were soon seen on the track post war. Some twenty-three GP racers were exported to the US from the factory, which also assisted the importers with limited production runs of T100/R models for 1955 and 1956, and then the T100RR for 1957 through to 1959. The 500cc bikes were competitive on

Typical ISDT equipment included a nail catcher to remove nails from the front tyre before they caused a puncture.

Triumph made much of winning in the USA. Here a magazine article celebrating wins at Catalina is reproduced as a brochure.

They're off!

This picture from the 1959 Triumph brochure gives an idea of the scale of a Big Bear race — hundreds of bikes setting off on a desert course.

the oval tracks and all through the 1950s, Triumph 500s competed against the 750cc Harley Davidson side valve bikes and 500cc BSA Gold Stars with some success.

Situated on the Island of Catalina, some 26 miles (42km) off the coast of Southern California, the Catalina Grand Prix was run from 1951 to 1958 and is often compared with the Isle of Man TT races. The island was owned by P K Wrigley, the chewing gum magnate, who also owned Triumph motorcycles and was happy to turn over the island to motor cycle racing for a weekend each year. There were two events, a 60-mile (97km) race for up to 250cc lightweights on the Saturday and a 100-mile (161km) race for bikes over 350cc was run on the Sunday. The course had every type of surface, from paved roads through the islands capital Avalon, to dirt tracks over its interior. The race was run in May, just in time for a win to provide good publicity for that year's selling season.

Triumphs competed in the event from the beginning and Walt Fulton won the first event on a 6T Thunderbird-derived racer. Victory then eluded the big Triumphs until 1955, when Bud Ekins won on a TR5. Bob Sandgren won the 1957 event on a TR6/B Trophybird and he repeated this feat in 1958, the event's final year.

Desert Racing

Post-World War Two, a new type of racing had emerged in the US. This was colloquially known as Desert Racing and comprised long distance cross-country races held in the open desert of the US southwest. In these competitions, large numbers of riders, more than 800 entries in the largest events, would go from a single starting line and follow a cross country 'course' that ran through the open desert and usually up and down any convenient mountain. Courses could be up to 500 miles (805km) long and a race could take all day to complete, often with many riders failing to finish through machine failure or rider fatigue. Held at a national and local level, these races were major tests of man and machine and winning provided a serious sales boost to the manufacturer of the victor's bike.

Major events included the Cactus Derby at between 250 to 440 miles length, the 500-mile Greenhorn Enduro and the 150-mile (241km) Big Bear, one of the most prestigious of the races. The Triumph TR6 was introduced to the US market in 1956, with four Trophies being uncrated and raced straight out of the box at that year's Big Bear enduro by Bud Ekins, Arvin Cox, Larry Hester and eventual winner Bill Postell.

The four riders lead the race from the start and finished in the first four places, giving Triumph incredible publicity and heralding its total domination of desert racing for the next ten years. The following year, TR6-mounted Bud Ekins won the Big Bear and Triumph took nine out of the first ten places, and twenty of the first twenty-five, giving it the most decisive win by places of a single manufacturer in a major post-World War Two US race. Success for Triumph TR6s in the Big Bear continued with Roger White winning in 1958 and Ekins clocking up his third Big Bear win in 1959, when nine Triumph TR6 riders took the first nine places.

The Greenhorn Run also became a Triumph benefit, with Bob Sothern winning on a TR5 in 1954. TR6-mounted Eddie Day won overall in 1957 and Buck Smith, again on a TR6, won overall in 1959. These victories in the big national races showed the TR6 to be the bike to have and stimulated sales to riders of all abilities who competed in the myriad of similar club-level events throughout the Western seaboard.

The Pre-unit Triumph in Production Racing

The Tiger 100, when combined with readily available tuning equipment and knowledge, made for a competitive and relatively cheap production racer throughout the 1950s, but it faced tough competition from the likes of BSA's Gold Star. However, in the 1950s a new type of endurance race for production machinery emerged, with the premier event being the Thruxton 500 miler. This new class of racing favoured larger capacity machines such as Triumph's 650. As the importance of the ISDT waned in the UK, in line with the success shown by British manufacturers, production racing started to take the imagination of the public and none more so than the Thruxton Nine Hours Endurance (later the 500-mile) race.

First held in 1955 at the Thruxton circuit in Hampshire, the race became a testing ground for the fast roadsters from British (and foreign) factories, and

As the 1950s came to an end, Triumph began competing in production racing. The Thruxton 500 mile race was the premier event in the UK, and the 1962 brochure celebrated Triumph's successes.

THRUXTON 500 MILE RACE
Outright winner of this arduous International Race for standard production motorcycles was a Triumph "Bonneville" ridden by Tony Godfrey and John Holder. Above is a fine view of Holder at speed on the winning machine. Other "Bonnevilles" filled 2nd, 4th, 5th and 6th places in the multicylinder class.

Triumph was there from the start. It fielded an iron-headed Tiger 110 in 1955, which failed to finish. The laurels were taken by a BSA Gold Star, while a Tiger 100 came in third. For 1956, four Tiger 100s and seven Tiger 110s were entered, and a Tiger 110 ridden by Percy Tait and Keith Bryen won the 750cc class, but the first six places all went to BSA Gold Stars. A Tiger 110 came second in the 1957 race and a similar machine eventually succeeded in winning the event in 1958, the winning machine being ridden by Mike Hailwood and Dan Shorey.

The announcement of the T120 Bonneville spelt the end of the Tiger 110 as Triumph's top sportster and the 1959 Thruxton event saw a T120 beaten into second place by a BMW R69. In 1960, T120 Bonnevilles finished second, third and fourth overall. Victory came to the Bonneville at the 1961 Thruxton 500 miler, however, with Tony Godfrey and John Holder coming in first. The use of the Pre-unit engine in production racing then started to fall off with the 500cc Unit bike becoming competitive and the emergence of the 650cc Unit engine in 1963.

Johnny Allen's Bonneville Speed run

The Triumph 650 engine was a versatile unit and a regular competitor at the speed trials held yearly at the Bonneville Salt Flats in Utah. The Bonneville Salt flats are formed when an enormous lake dries out over the summer months, leaving a huge flat area covered in a hard crust of dry salt, where cars and motor cycles can do speed runs for a couple of weeks each year.

Probably the most famous Triumph-powered machine to run on the flats was the streamliner initially called 'The Devils Arrow' and later renamed 'Texas Cee-gar'. Built in 1954 by Texas airline captain Stormy Mangham, the bike had a custom made tubular chassis enclosed in a streamliner shell and was powered by a naturally aspirated, methanol-burning Triumph 6T engine tuned by the legendary Jack Wilson. The bike was long at 188in (4775mm), but slim at a mere 22_in (570mm) wide. It was piloted by Johnny Allen, a racer from Fort Worth, Texas.

It came good in 1955, and on 25 September set the highest speeds ever achieved by a motor cycle at Bon-

Allen's streamliner was powered by a naturally-aspirated Thunderbird engine, albeit heavily tuned.

Johnny Allen's record breaking run with a streamliner at Bonneville warranted its own brochure.

Allen's restored streamliner is currently on display at the UK's National Motorcycle Museum.

A jaunty Johnny Allen poses on his Tiger 100.

Johnny Allen poses on another
of his record breaking Triumphs
—a 500 c.c. Tiger 100.

neville, turning in a flying mile at 192.3mph (309.5km/h) and a flying kilometre at 193.72mph (311.76km/h), with the record confirmed by the American Motorcycle Association (AMA), the sport's controlling body. However, there was some question as to whether this record would be ratified by the Fédération Internationale de Motocyclisme (FIM), the international motor sport regulator, since it had no reciprocal agreement with the AMA. The FIM set up an enquiry to investigate, but before the record could be ratified it was beaten by NSU at Bonneville in 1956, with a run of 210.64mph (338.99km/h). But Allen returned to the salt and on 6 September 1956 regained the record at an amazing 214.7mph (345.4km/h). This record was ratified by the AMA, but NSU raised a query since the official FIM time-keeper had left Bonneville before Allen's run. Even though the timekeeper had handed over authority to an AMA official, NSU claimed that this was a breach of FIM rules and the record should not be ratified. All this led to a long drawn out FIM enquiry and the eventual result was that the FIM refused to ratify Allen's record, despite there being no doubt that the speed had been reached. All this resulted in a great deal of publicity for Triumph, which was happy to have the AMA endorsement for the record; the US was a big market and the whole affair reflected badly on the FIM. Triumph capitalised on the affair by proclaiming they were the world record holder and from then on all new Triumphs carried a transfer with the Thunderbird logo and the words 'World Motorcycle Record Holder' on them.

Competition Summary

Considering that Triumph's competition units were firmly based on production engines, its Pre-unit twin bikes were very successful in certain areas of motor sport. Bearing in mind the production origins of the unit, it is not surprising that the Triumphs were only briefly successful in the heady world of Grand Prix racing, but in production racing the Triumph was the bike to beat, with an unparalleled mix of power, light-

Pre-unit Triumph racers still emerge today. This unusual example was spotted at a recent Kempton autojumble.

Triumph Pre-unit engines were also used in UK off-road competition. This is a Rickman Metisse-framed Tiger 100 scrambler.

weight and reliability. In conjunction with easily available information on engine tuning and factory supplied race kits, the Pre-unit was competitive throughout (and after) its production life.

Off road the Triumph was successful in the 1940s and 1950s at an international level, in events such as the ISDT, while Triumph 650s were the bikes to beat in US desert racing events all through the 1950s, with the Unit Construction models continuing to be competitive through the 1960s.

Triumph-engined streamliners and 'standard' bikes continued to perform at Bonneville after Johnny Allen's record breaking run. All in all the Pre-unit Triumph made competitive machinery available to the man in the street, and that is a pretty good legacy and one that Triumph should be proud of.

CHAPTER 5

OWNING AND RIDING

Owning and riding a Pre-unit Triumph is rewarding and many owners retain a deep rooted affection for the machines. Some appreciate the lazy, relaxed nature of the Speed Twin and Thunderbird, others prefer the more performance orientated Tiger 100, Tiger 110 and Bonneville. All Triumph owners appreciate the bikes and how they reward their owners with a solid and trustworthy ride.

Tony Sumner's 6T Thunderbird

Tony Sumner, a school friend of the author, has owned his Triumph Thunderbird since 1974. Tony bought the bike in bits when he was 16, with the intention of putting it on the road when he passed his motor cycle test and he succeeded in this aim. The bike was a rigid framed, sprung hub 1954 model, complete with the optional dual seat rather than a single seat and bum pad. Largely original, it featured that year's nacelle and the relatively weedy half-width 7in front brake, 1in diameter handlebars and the 'Rev-o-lator' speedometer. The only downside to the bike when Tony bought it was that it was in pieces.

Tony set to in a caravan in his back garden and by the time he passed his test the Triumph was ready to go. I still remember him showing me the partially dismantled sprung hub with its cast-in warning notice. Luckily Tony knew the risks inherent in the sprung hub and its tightly constrained springs, and did not want any extra holes appearing in the caravan roof or, indeed, him.

Tony brush painted all the cycle parts using Dulux gloss enamel, getting the paint colour matched to the original Triumph Polychromatic Blue. The paint itself was a solid colour and actually looked pretty good – the original Dulux is still on the bike today. The dual seat was Triumph's own Twin seat, which Tony recovered and did a very professional looking job on. All in all, the completed bike looked really good, if a little old fashioned. And it went well too...

Tony had passed his test on a 175cc Montessa Impala, which was an impressively quick single cylinder two stroke that could give a British 350cc bike a run for its money. A Bantam it was not, but with its peaky power delivery and high revving motor, it was very different in character to the big Triumph. Despite this contrast, Tony found the Thunderbird easy to handle and ride. He found its relatively low seat height an asset (Tony is not the tallest of guys) and the softly tuned engine with bags of low end torque made for an easy and relaxing ride.

By T'bird to Wales

Tony and the author took their bikes on holiday in 1977, the author on his 1971 BSA B25SS 250cc single and Tony on the T'bird. Starting from Tony's home in Yateley, Hampshire, we were aiming to meet up with friends who had a holiday cottage at Newgale in West Wales. This meant a run of some 240 miles (386km). We could not use the direct motorway route since I had not passed my test, but this meant we cruised through some lovely countryside in the south of England, through the Cotswolds and into Wales on the old main roads, and both the B25SS and the Thunderbird excelled on these roads.

Tony Sumner and his 6T Thunderbird, somewhere in Wales in the 1970s.

The author enjoys a beer on his T25SS, in front of Tony's Thunderbird.

The route we took had probably not changed much since the Thunderbird was built. These were the relatively fast 'A' roads that the Thunderbird was designed for and it coped with them admirably. In fact, my bike provided the only drama en route, when it wouldn't restart after a lunch break in Abergavenny. The Thunderbird just kept on running, without drama, and handled the return journey with similar style.

The only time I remember Tony having trouble was on a wet afternoon when we were taking a short-cut home that involved the ford in Eversley. It had been raining a lot and the water level in the ford was quite high, but Tony decided to press on. I stopped – despite my B25SS having massive ground clearance and a relatively waterproofed engine and electrics – and watched Tony plough on through the torrent. When the water was almost at the top of his boots he suddenly stopped and put one hand on the engine while the other punched the kill button on the nacelle. I ran into the ford and between us we pulled the bike out backwards. He explained that he when he saw that the water level was over the timing cover he realised that he had to stop to avoid getting water sucked into the engine via the unfiltered carburettor. So he quickly had to put one hand over the carburettor's air intake to keep the water out while he killed the engine.

With just a few kicks the bike started, despite the magneto having been pretty much submerged. Apart from the bike ejecting two silencer loads of water over my already sodden trousers, it ran okay. So we heaved a sigh of relief and with no damage done we turned round and went home the long way.

The bike was Tony's prime transport while he was at school and when he went up to Imperial College, London, to read physics. It became a common site chuffing around the capital for the three years that Tony lived there.

My overwhelming impression of the Thunderbird is of a gentle bike. It is not highly strung or highly tuned, it is mechanically very quiet with its all-iron top end, is relatively oil leak free and it is in a lovely soft state of tune. It is perfectly capable of gently bimbling around, but had the ability and performance if you opened the throttle to show a clean pair of heels to many younger bikes and cars. The faithful steed now lives in Tony's shed in Cambridge, where it shares the space with a portfolio (that's the new trendy word for a collection of old bikes) of other clunkers. Tony is now considering restoring it, but should he put the bike back to standard or how it was when he was riding it in his teenage years?

Ken Moorhouse's T100 – then and now

Ken Moorhouse owned a T100 back in the 1960s and during that time owned a number of bikes, including an Excelsior Talisman twin, a Douglas Plus 90, Vincent Comet, Triumph Twenty-one and BSA Shooting Star. However, apart from the BSA (which he regrets selling), he was not overly impressed with the performance of the other bikes and gravitated to a 1955 Tiger 100. It cost him a mere £60, which sounds good today, but he was an apprentice at the time and earning only few pounds a week, so it represented a major investment. The bike was a good runner, but not so good cosmetically; the fuel tank had been repainted grey, with the rest of the cycle parts in blue. He had to put new tyres on it, but otherwise it was running well when he bought it.

The performance was the main thing that impressed Ken at the time. It was very good in comparison to the other bikes (although the Shooting Star was close) and it coped with two-up riding while he was courting his wife-to-be Margaret with no problem. In fact, Margaret became a permanent pillion fixture on the Tiger when Ken married her. Ken and Margaret found the Tiger comfortable and used it for a number of holidays and general days out.

Ken did his national service in the RAF and was stationed in Calne for some of that time. He spent many Friday and Sunday evenings thundering up and down the A4 to get to and from his parents house in Essex – a trip of some 150 miles (241km) – and this put many thousands of miles on the Tiger. These late night/early morning runs remain among Ken's fondest memories of the bike. In those pre-speed limit times he could cruise comfortably at 80mph (129km/h) with the occasional blast up to 90mph (145km/h) when required. The road would be deserted and the lights on the bike were good, making for an enjoyable and exhilarating ride. Performance-wise, Ken was impressed. While he never took it flat out, he saw 90 indicated on many occasions, with more to come.

Ken Moorhouse on his new Tiger 100.

Acceleration in the gears was very good and he can remember seeing 75 mph in third gear on occasions, sometimes two up. The brakes, with the big 8in unit on the front, were good and never gave him any cause for concern. Mechanically it was fine, although he did partially strip the engine once, using the facilities of a friend's garage. Ken can't remember why it needed this treatment, but it wasn't serious. What was serious was that he was supposed to be seeing Margaret that evening and had to be dragged home by his Dad at 3am, having missed his date!

Minor Mishaps

On one occasion the bike almost let him down. He and Margaret had ridden out to Clacton for the day. Stopping at a garage for fuel, Ken suddenly became aware that both of them had hot boots on the right hand side. One of the oil pipes had split, pouring hot oil over their feet. It must have happened as they pulled into the garage. It was an easily fixed issue, which was luckily caught in time, so no damage was done to the engine.

The only other mechanical malady Ken can remember was the bike's appetite for rear spokes.

Ken's Tiger has later fork sliders with bolt-on caps – this is one of the features he plans to change.

Ken's Tiger 100 engine is a fine sight.

Once he lost two at the Dome Garage coming out of London and had to take it really easy down the A4 to Calne. Luckily it was easy to fix and all was sorted during the week, ready for the fast run home the following weekend. Ken's worst moment on the bike was riding straight over the Beckhampton roundabout on the A4 at around 2am one morning while heading back to Calne. He thinks he must have fallen asleep on the bike. Little damage was done, just slightly bent forks and a broken brake lever, and luckily no damage to Ken. He was able to continue the ride back to base and the bike was easily fixed in time for the Friday run home.

Ken was so happy with the Tiger that he regretted selling it, but the needs of a family and the comfort and convenience of a car eventually won and he sold the bike to pay for his honeymoon. It was sold for £75, making a £15 profit. That's what a three-day honeymoon in Devon cost in 1961; the RAF only allowed three days off.

Ken has recently bought another Tiger 100, a 1956 model that he is currently shaking down and sorting out. It is as he remembers, light, good handling and with super performance, combined with a smooth and tractable engine. So far he has had a great time fettling and the bike is bringing back many happy memories of the 1960s.

Peter Horwood's T110 and Steib Sidecar

Peter Horwood is a lifelong motorcyclist who currently rides a Morini. Back in the early 1960s he ran a 1948 Speed Twin for a couple of years as his ride into work in central London from Sidcup. It never let him down and he replaced it with a 1958 Tiger 110 in black and white with a sporting Steib sidecar in 1962. The Tiger 110, like the Speed Twin, was his daily transport – but only after he had lost faith in a James Cadet when it caught fire. Peter had just filled it up with petrol and two-stroke oil mixture and kicked it over when the flywheel cover blew off and the whole bike burst into flames. Peter had to shoo passing school children away from the conflagration while a kind soul from the garage threw a bucket of sand over the bike, which put it out, but it was never the same after the incident!

In contrast to the James, the Triumph never malfunctioned. He ran the Tiger 110 for some four or five years until he had to sell it to buy a car, since he had children coming along. He rode the bike everywhere, taking it to Scotland and Devon on holiday, as well as using it for the daily commute. Peter found the performance of the bike with its sports sidecar to be very good and he had no handling problems or major mechanical issues with it. The only problem he remembers was on a summer holiday trip to Scotland, when the clutch cable broke. Luckily the bike had the Slickshift gearbox, so Peter was able to nurse it along without the clutch cable until he found a Triumph dealer who could supply a new cable.

Peter found the bike fast considering it was a combination, and its good handling and performance meant that it could happily outperform most other vehicles on the road at the time. While the Speed Twin was just another bike to Peter, the Tiger 110 made a lasting impression on him and he remembers it fondly.

Peter Horwood's T110 and Steib, pictured at Regents Park, London, in 1962.

Peter's lovely T110, back in the day…

*Peter's later T110 sported a siamesed
exhaust system.*

Bruce Simpson's Tiger 110 and Trophy TR5

Bruce Simpson is a serial bike restorer and noted Scott expert, but the bike that started his collection was a 1961 Tiger 110, the machine that he has owned longest in his entire collection. The bike was despatched to Harpers Garage in Gloucestershire in September 1960 and Bruce bought it in 1971, in oily rag, but running condition. He rode it for a number of years but in the late 1990s decided that it was time to restore it. When he bought the bike it was a 1972 Bonneville look-a-like – with oil in frame breadbox tank and chromed headlamp – but luckily the previous owner had given Bruce the original 'Bathtub', petrol tank and nacelle. Bruce had kept the metalwork dry and safe for the 20 odd years he had owned the bike. The Tiger also has its original engine and frame (with all-important matching numbers) and the original gearbox with Slickshift.

The rebuild was completed with few dramas; the engine needed a rebore and a regrind and received new main bearings while it was apart. The gearbox was stripped and found to be in fine condition, with no replacement parts needed, so the cases were cleaned and the outer cover lightly polished. With the mechanicals sorted the frame was treated to a blasting and a powder coat in black, and the wheels were treated to stainless rims and spokes.

The engine received a new Monobloc carburettor. Bruce has found that while you can rebuild old Amal carburettors, replacing the originals with new ones has invariably improved the running of his rebuilds and with the easy availability of new units he would not contemplate a refurbishment any more, an opinion that reflects the author's experience. One departure from standard was the fitting of a Haywood belt drive. Bruce reckons that this is one of the best things he did, since it made the engine run much more smoothly and quietly.

Since the bike was a 'Bathtub' model with a lot of surface area to be painted, Bruce was careful who he chose to do the paintwork. He trusted it to local sprayer Mike Easey, based out in the sticks between Crondel and Bentley in North Hampshire. Mike did an excellent job of both matching the Triumph colours and producing a fault-free finish.

The proof of the quality of the Tiger 110 restoration came with a first prize in the July 1998 Yateley Carnival, a third at the August 2000 Triumph Owners Club Berkshire Branch show at the Tadley Rugby Club, and a first prize at the 2003 Fleet Carnival Run.

Bruce really likes the bike and the way it rides. He has Avon tyres on it, a ribbed front and SM rear, and finds that they suit the Tiger and provide a good, confidence-inspiring feel to its handling. With its completely refurbished front and rear suspension the bike goes around corners as if it were 'on rails'. Bruce likes it a lot and finds it just great to sit on and ride! And the best thing about it? When he rides it through town everyone looks round!

Bruce's other Pre-unit Triumph is a 1953 Triumph Trophy. He bought it from a friend early in 2009 – he'd known the bike for a while and really fancied it. While Bruce did not restore it, he rates it as one of his favourite bikes, due to its combination of light weight, manoeuvrability and flexibility. As Bruce put it, the Trophy is:

> A wonderful bike to ride, it's got everything you need on a bike apart from brakes! The engine is beautiful, the gearbox is slick – well it's a Triumph – and it's such a reliable engine as well. It's smooth, with trials gearing, the maintenance is low, and it always starts second kick. The bike is something else, it feels good, rides good and does you good!

All these attributes are, of course, a result of Turner's genius in designing a bike that was uniquely suited to the competition demands of the late 1940s and early 1950s, which resulted in a machine that fitted the way Bruce rides today down to a 'T' – where the 'T' stands for Trophy.

The bike has a lot of history with it, originally being built up by a previous owner (now deceased) from parts, and having a generator-type engine fitted. It has been joked that while the majority of the bits making up the bike came from Meriden, they didn't necessarily come out of the factory at the same time. Several years ago the Trophy was treated to a genuine 1953 TR5 engine unit, with its number just a few hundred later than the frame, so it now has a TR5 frame and engine, which makes it a real Trophy in the author's eyes. A previous keeper recounted the bike's recent history in the June 2006 issue of *RealClassic* magazine.

When Bruce Simpson bought his T110 it had a 1970s' Bonneville 'Breadbox' fuel tank.

Chromed mudguards and a 1968 twin leading shoe front brake were also non-standard.

Bruce has ridden and exhibited the machine over the last couple of years and has found it to be an excellent day-to-day rider. With its trail/trials gearing the bike is peppy and responsive, and at the typical speed of classic runs in Bruce's neck of the woods, ultimate top end performance is not needed. The only work Bruce had done to the bike was to repair a dent in the front mudguard and have the mudguard repainted. He also replaced the carburettor with a new one, making the bike much better behaved, with a steady and reliable tick over and cleaner pickup than before. The cylinder head is at the time of writing (2011) receiving attention as the exhaust ports were starting to blow, and he found that the threads have stripped — they had gone before and at some stage thread inserts had been used to repair them, but these had pulled out again. However, Bruce is working on a permanent solution and will soon have the old warhorse back on the road. After all he can't miss a summer without riding his favourite steed.

Bruce's restoration put back the 'Bathtub' and original nacelle.

Bruce's Tiger 110 is a show winner. It looks superb.

Bruce Simpson's Trophy has the close-finned T100-style alloy barrel and head.

One of Bruce's favourite bikes, the Trophy is pictured here on a run in 2010.

The Trophy still has the chromed tank and Triumph's famous tank rack.

Eric Coombs T120 Prototype

Eric Coombs is a Triumph man and owns, among others, a 1969 Bonneville. Back in 2002 a work colleague asked him if he would be interested in a Triumph Bonneville that had belonged to his father-in-law, who had passed away. As is the way of these things, the colleague then decided to rebuild the bike himself, but found the job too much. About a year later he asked Eric if he was still interested, so Eric had a look. He saw that the cases were stamped T120, but that the engine number was in the 190xx range, when all the documented evidence said that Bonneville's numbers began at 20,000. Eric made him an offer, but on the basis that he could carry out some research to confirm that it was a Bonneville, and not a tarted-up Tiger 110. The vendor had documentation, including a duplicate logbook, and this was enough for Eric to make the purchase.

Eric Coombs aboard his pre-production Bonneville prototype.

Eric's T120 looks the part in Blue over Pearl Grey.

Eric did a dry build of the bike in his garage to see what he actually had, and this showed him that it was virtually all there, although it was missing its original front mudguard – an alloy unit came with it. Other than this the bike seemed pretty much complete and original. Eric then decided to continue with his research into the machine's history and it remained in its loosely built up state for several years. Eric's research uncovered the fact that it was a local bike, registered at Trowbridge. The father-in-law of the vendor had bought it from another local, who had bought it from his brother, who bought it in 1963 when he part exchanged a Tiger Cub for the Bonneville. Here the trail went cold, but the man who bought it in 1963 can tantalisingly identify the row of houses that he bought it from and remembers that it was advertised in the *Wiltshire Times* or the *Bath Chronicle*. Eric can't tie the bike down to a particular name or address, however. He has searched the *Wiltshire Times* and in 2011 was still checking the *Bath Chronicle* for the advert, but so far with no luck; his investigations are continuing!

Further research through the Triumph Owners Motor Cycle Club (TOMCC) and Richard Wheedon (the TOMCC registrar) showed that the bike did appear in the Triumph despatch records. The bike was despatched on 25 October 1958 – the same day it was registered – to Pankhurst Ltd in Yeovil, in keeping with the Trowbridge registration. Pankhurst was one of the biggest Triumph dealers in the West Country at the time. Further perusal of the despatch record showed the bike to be identified as a T120, and that the engine and frame number was at the end of a run of T110s. The engine number is stamped T120, but close inspection of the stamping shows that it may be possible that the '2' in 'T120' had been stamped over the '1' in T110. However, the dispatch record showed that the batch of Tiger 110s in the manufacturing run prior to Eric's was despatched in June 1958, as were the bikes after Eric's example, and the records show Eric's as a T120, although again the '2' looks to have been written over a '1' in the record. So it looks like Eric's machine was plucked from the production line for some special reason and kept by the factory between June and October 1958, then despatched as a 'normal' production model T120. The engine build record also shows that it was fitted with a pair of E3134 cams, a racing magneto and high compression pistons, so the engine was never actually built to standard Tiger 110 specification, which again points to the bike being something special.

Detailed examination of the bike also gives some indication that it is in fact the bike featured in a number of original factory photographs reproduced in books, such as Jeff Clew's *Turners Triumphs* and John Nelson's *Bonnie*. As well as the indications mentioned, the photos show that the pre-production prototype's oil tank lacked the froth tower and that the toolbox/air filter intake was cut about to allow for the fitting of the separate carburettor float bowl and Eric's bike displayed both these characteristics. Eric's conclusion is that the bike was, in all likelihood, a pre-production machine used to finalise the Bonneville production build and so can legitimately be called a pre-production Bonneville.

The T120 pre-production prototype has a remote float bowl and chopped Monobloc carburettors.

Restoration

When he came to restore the bike, Eric had only a few pictures of the machine from the 1970s, when it was painted all over in white, with what seemed to be a 'Dulux special' paint job. When he came to strip it down, the only trace of original paint he could find was a cream colour on the rear mudguard. The 1963 owner had painted it, but could only remember that it was a blue-grey colour and couldn't give any details. So Eric had no evidence of the original finish, but he did have the various black and white pictures of the bike. He got a good friend, John Kettle, a retired BBC cameraman, to do an analysis of the pictures and from this he came to the conclusion that the colour scheme was as the bike is now painted – interestingly, the analysis showed that the nacelle was not black but in fact the same colour as the oil tank. Combined with the previous owner remembering the 'bluey-grey' colour, Eric decided on the Blue over Pearl Grey scheme and very nice it looks too.

Eric had a lot of help from Dave Franklin, another good friend, who is extremely knowledgeable about Pre-unit Triumphs and had rebuilt the National Motor-cycle Museum's original Speed Twin. Eric doesn't think he has met anyone who knows more about Pre-units and Dave spent a few days helping Eric with the build.

Basically the rebuild was straightforward, with Eric stripping the bike down after a dry rebuild ready for the paint. The only missing parts were the front mudguard – Eric sourced a Tiger 110 unit – and the gearbox, which Eric replaced with a non-Slickshift Bonneville item. It was a pity that the original did not come with the bike, since not all Bonnevilles had the Slickshift mechanism, while all Tiger 110s did, and that could have been another indication of the bike's provenance. Another interesting point was that a previous owner had used grub screws in the rocker boxes to hold the rocker covers in place – Eric replaced them with alloy inserts. Another issue was trying to find someone to do the cadmium plating on all the nuts and bolts, and other parts. Hockley Engineering in Essex was eventually recommended and the company did a splendid job without losing any of the bits he sent them.

The only disappointing part of the restoration was that the first painting was poor. Eric was not happy with the workmanship and had to have all of the paint re-done. The new work was done by Joeby's Airbrush Art, situated just outside Wells and Eric cannot recommend 'Joeby' highly enough for the quality of the work and his attention to detail – including his hand painted sign writing and pin striping. The bike won best in show at the 2011 Bristol Classic Motor Cycle Show against stiff competition and this shows the quality and thoroughness of Eric's restoration and research.

Eric likes the bike, even if he is, in his own words, 'a unit man'. He feels a connection with it since it is the same age as his wife, Shirley, and its registration letters are SHR. All in all Eric has done a magnificent job in rescuing a bike with a fascinat-ing pedigree. Without his research and dedication to detail it would have been perfectly possible that the machine could have been restored as either a T110 or a T120 and all references to its unique history lost or never uncovered.

The engine looks every inch a T120 unit and the gearbox is a non-Slickshift item.

The quality of Eric's restoration shines through.

Paul Mansfield's TRW

The TRW may seem a strange choice for a Triumph rider and enthusiast, but Paul Mansfield of the Berkshire branch of the TOMCC is thoroughly entranced by his example. While in performance terms it is a million miles away from a T120 Bonneville or Tiger 100, the no nonsense and fuss-free ride it provides is perfect for pootling along the Berkshire back lanes around where Paul lives.

Paul bought his TRW in 2000. It is an ex-RAF model that had spent all its service life in Cyprus, before ending up in Scotland in pieces.

Paul had picked up a TRW engine quite cheaply at the Kempton Autojumble in October 2000. He saw the engine on the ground and didn't recognise it with its cast-in inner primary chain case. Asking the stallholder what it was, he was told that it was a Triumph TRW unit and bought it on the spot for £130. He then found another, still crated, at another jumble. It bore the number before his, so he had to buy that one as well. This pair of engines had wetted his appetite for TRWs and he began collect parts as they turned up, as well as researching the model. He placed a wanted advert for TRW parts in *Classic Bike Guide* magazine, which resulted in a gentleman from Scotland ringing him and asking him what he needed. When Paul asked him what he had, he told him that he had a complete TRW in bits. Paul bought it. He drove up to Culloden, near Loch Ness, picked up the boxes of parts and was back in his workshop near Reading, Berkshire, after a 1,200-mile (1,931km) round trip by 3:00pm, when he began stripping the bits down. He had start off quite early mind...

The bike currently has the 1952 engine that Paul bought still in its purpose-made crate from Kempton, with a Miller alternator and BT-H magneto, and a standard wide ratio gearbox. Paul rebuilt everything, frame, running gear, forks, engine and gearbox to bring the bike up to its present immaculate condition, both cosmetically and mechanically. Devon based Tri-Supply was singled out as an excellent source of spares and help – everything Paul bought from the company fitted.

The Ride

Paul loves the low seat height (despite having a higher Speed Twin-type saddle fitted), which means you can relax at traffic lights with both feet on the ground. The handling with the Trophy-type frame is not like that of a modern bike. Paul finds it goes round bends easily, but it doesn't like roundabouts and the quick changes of direction they need. But overall he finds the bike comfortable, despite the rigid back end. With the wide ratio gearbox the bike goes off the mark like a 'scalded cat' and he has seen 80mph (129km/h). Paul feels there's a bit more in the machine, but chickened out when he reached 80' and has found that the comfortable cruising speed is 45mph (72km/h) – Paul's idea of heaven is a steady cruise to a pub on a summer's evening. The brakes he found variable. The back brake is quite good, which is just as well, since the front is awful: 'you might as well not bother with it!' says Paul. He replaced the original Solex carburettor with a 26mm Amal Concentric after the Solex let him down with blocked jets. This fitted without any problems and performs well.

Paul takes an interest in TRWs and his research has uncovered a couple of useful points. Firstly, Triumph developed alloy barrels for the early TRWs, which were used on the bikes supplied to The White Helmets – the Royal Signals Display team – and has pictures of trials TRWs fitted with alloy barrels. One of the trials bikes with the alloy barrels also had an Amal Concentric and a magneto, which meant that it needed a long inlet manifold for the carburettor to clear the mag. Secondly, he points out the differences between the early BT-H alternator equipped bikes and the later Lucas machines. The BT-H bikes had the output wires from the chain case-fitted alternator routed out of the top of the chain case, while the Lucas-equipped TRWs had a different casting, with the wires coming out of the back and this meant they employed different crankcase castings, since the front rear of the primary chain case is cast in one with the drive side crankcase.

Paul wants to keep his TRW for a long time and he has been collecting parts as time goes by. In fact, he has three spare engines, numerous gearboxes and parts, and is starting to think about building up another example. Originally he was going to convert his TRW into a green laner, but he likes the largely

Paul Mansfield's TRW was a non-standard yellow in its early days. Here it is loosely assembled shortly after he bought it.

Now all together and on the road, the TRW is finished in an attractive blue.

The rigid rear end (no sprung hub on this TRW) makes for a lively ride, but the long saddle springs absorb all but the worst road shocks.

standard look – it's quite 'bobberish', as he describes it – and he may just raid his spares stock and build up a second bike to be the green laner.

Paul's best time with the TRW was a ride over the Berkshire downs to West Hagbourne, for a bike meet held there early one July evening. Riding through the countryside at a gentle 40mph (64km/h), with the poppy fields in bloom, the sun shining and in the knowledge that he was going to see some nice bikes at a nice pub was just heavenly.

An Amal Concentric carburettor replaced the original Solex unit, which was prone to blocked jets.

TRWs are popular in pre-1965 trials – this one has a set of alloy barrels.

Chris Bunce's ex-Police 1958 Speed Twin

Chris Bunce is the proprietor of Classic SuperBikes, based in Fleet, Hampshire. One of the bikes he had in stock at the time of writing was a 1958 Speed Twin. He bought it from a gentleman called Mike Berry, sadly now deceased, whom he met when he went to see a BSA B31 he had for sale. To cut a long story short, Chris eventually bought Mr Berry's small collection of bikes, along with various spares. One of these machines was the 1958 Speed Twin. Chris had ridden the Speed Twin when he first got it and while it didn't make much of an initial impression, it slowly grew on him.

The history of the Speed Twin also captured Chris's attention. It was originally despatched from Meriden on 30 May 1958 to be delivered to Essex Constabulary, via Hadlers Garage, Chelmsford, Essex, and was one of a batch of nine Speed Twins delivered at the time. It was subsequently sold off at auction at the time of the 1973 fuel crisis, but was little used and Mike Berry bought it later that year. At the time Mike ran a vintage car dealership in North London. When he got the 5T it was still in police trim, with the single saddle and special extra battery carrier, and so had no drive side panel. Wanting to convert the bike to civilian spec, Mike went to Moore's of Tottenham, a big London Triumph dealer, to get a seat and side panel. When he got there he found that Moore's was clearing out all its Pre-unit stock of spares, so he bought a complete front end, seat, fuel tank and side panel, and an assortment of other parts, all in Amaranth red and original factory wrappings. Mike put the bike in his dealership's workshop and set his lads to overhaul it and replace all the cycle parts with the new parts – note that the tank is a pre-1957 unit, with the four bar Triumph badge. He then kept and rode the bike sparingly, until he sold it to Chris in 2010.

When Chris got the bike he sent it to his Triumph specialist where he had the Slickshift gearbox adjusted and the clutch pushrod replaced. He then had a call from Mike asking Chris to give him a hand to clear out one of his garages. When Chris obliged they found the original police spotlights, with blue centre, and a set of brand new 'Patrol' leg shields, complete with fit-

Chris Bunce's ex-police Speed Twin looks the part, with its period leg shields and blue lights.

The nacelle has an original 'Speed Twin' decal.

tings. Chris is unsure if the leg shields originally came with the bike, or if they were part of the spares cache Mike bought from Moore's, but he fitted them and the lights to his bike. A nice touch is the chrome period fire extinguisher, also rescued from Mike's garage, clipped to the left hand leg shield.

An interesting feature of the bike is its dual charging system. A standard 1958 5T would have been equipped with an alternator and coil ignition. Chris's bike has the alternator and coil ignition system, but also has a dynamo and the associated wiring, to help power the extra lights and radio that would have equipped the police bike. A final touch was Chris managing to get the original registration number back from DVLA – when Mike bought the bike he had put a personalised registration number on it.

As Chris delved into the Speed Twin's history and rode it on a number of local classic bike events, he become more enamoured with it. He likes its easy personality and the way it just lollops along. While the performance is not spectacular and there is no discernable power band, Chris loves the sheer effortlessness of the way the bike performs. It runs beautifully smoothly and the brakes work better than those of most Triumphs of the era that Chris has tried. The bike also handles very well on its 1970s Dunlop TT100s. Its comfortable cruising speed is around 60mph (97km/h). At that speed there is 'some in reserve' and the bike feels happy. It is willing to buzz up to higher speeds and happy accelerating to over 70mph (113km/h), although Chris hasn't experimented above that speed. He also appreciates the Slickshift gearbox, especially when changing down and indicating, but doesn't feel that it adds much to the overall experience. Chris just loves the bike as it is, with its history and super riding characteristics, and is going to hang onto it and use it for a long time in Mike Berry's memory.

The 'Patrol' brand leg shields have their original paint and manufacturer's decals.

Chris Bunce astride his favourite bike.

Chris's Speed Twin ready to go!

Rodark Panniers

Among the most distinctive accessories made for bikes in the 1950s and early 1960s were Rodark Panniers. In contrast to many aftermarket panniers that were made in wood or glass fibre, the Rodarks were made entirely in steel and, rather than being plain boxes, they had a curved quarter-circle profile that matched the lines of virtually any bike; they looked especially good on a Pre-unit Triumph. There was a reason for this suitability, since the manufacturer used original Triumph mudguard pressings to form the top and rear sections of the panniers. The mudguard pressing was hinged at its bottom and there was a neat lock on the top to secure the lid. The inside of the case had a flat plate to the rear to stop the rider's goods and chattels from spilling out when the lid was opened, and there was a neat lip around the opening to keep the rain out – how successful this was is open to question! While the shape did compromise carrying capacity, the panniers made a welcome change from the style-free box-like units or ex-army kit bags previously available, and were robust and tough. With a matching paint job they integrated well with any bike.

The panniers were made by J J Couches Ltd, based in St Ives, Cornwall. The author talked with Clive B Taylor, who created the tooling to produce the panniers, and he revealed that the mudguard pressings were genuine Triumph. They were rolled, then endplates were cut and welded onto them, before hinges were fitted at the bottom to form the lids. All components were hand filed and gas welded. The firm used a 100-ton Horden, Mason & Edwards power press with a large die cushion to form and draw the pannier main panel from one piece of steel sheet. This was then formed into a box using a fly press and spot welded to form the pannier body, onto which the lids were attached. The company had its own painting booths and infrared ovens and water screens and, of course, matching paints for every motor cycle of the time. Indeed, the factory could prepare a set of panniers entirely in-house and paint them to match virtually any bike.

Rodarks are a sought after accessory today, since they are still both stylish and reasonably practical. With the right finish they enhance any classic bike and second-hand examples can be found in the classifieds or on Internet auction sites. And, of course, they are the perfect period accessory for a touring Thunderbird or Speed Twin.

Clive B. Taylor on his 250cc Royal Enfield, with Rodark panniers.

This fully equipped Tiger 100 is on display at the National Motorcycle Museum.

The lids of Rodark panniers were formed using the same tooling as the Triumph rear mudguards.

This lovely Rodark-equipped T110 was pictured at Amberley.

The Rodarks were very stylish, but could be awkward to load. Note the built-in stay and lock.

Police Pre-Units

The Metropolitan Police was early user of the Speed Twin, taking delivery of 24 Amaranth Red examples in 1938. While publicity stated this was the result of exhaustive tests by the Engineers Department of New Scotland Yard of many British manufacturers' products, Ivor Davies, in his book *It's Easy on a Triumph*, recounts how the Speed Twin was not ready at the beginning of the test process, but Turner persuaded the testers to try it towards the end of the process and it came out top. When the Thunderbird was introduced, it was also adopted, as were the higher performance 650s, throughout the 1950s.

The 5T became a favourite of many UK police forces in the post-war years and the Amaranth Red bikes soon became a familiar sight on Britain's roads. Triumph also enjoyed considerable export success, especially in Commonwealth countries such as Australia. The famous Triumph Saint (Stop Anything in No Time) model was a Unit Construction 650cc bike, introduced in the mid-1960s as a standard police specification model with specially tuned engine, and fairing, seat and other police equipment fitted at the factory. Before the introduction of the Saint, the factory did not have a standard police model, rather the bikes were either supplied as standard models for police workshops, or local dealers to modify, or the factory would build a specific batch to a required specification for a particular force.

Typical equipment of a Pre-unit police bike included radios and specially adopted fuel tanks to fit them, single seats, radio racks, panniers, leg shields, windscreens and extra lights. The bikes enjoyed a fine reputation and great popularity with the various forces. They were generally considered reliable, with good performance and the ability to get the job done.

TOP LEFT: *A period shot of a 5T Speed Twin leading a later, Unit Construction, 650 at Hendon.*

ABOVE: *Chris Bunce's 5T showing typical police-issue leg shields and fire extinguisher.*

LEFT: *Despite its dual seat, Chris Bunce's 5T has its police-issue lights and leg shields.*

BIBLIOGRAPHY AND SOURCES

More books have probably been written about Triumph motor cycles than the bikes of any other British manufacturer and this in itself is a testament to their popularity. The following books are all in my library and I have dipped in and out of most of them while producing this history. Many transport museums have motor cycle collections and will usually have a Triumph or two, but the five identified below contain significant bikes and I have included photographs of various of their exhibits in this book. Finally, the Internet is an invaluable source of data for the Triumph enthusiast and I have identified some of the better sites that I have seen.

Ayton, Cyril, compiled and introduced by, *Triumph Twins from 1937* (Bay View Books, ISBN 1-870979-17-6). Comprises a brief introduction and reprints of road tests and features from The Motor Cycle and Motor Cycling magazines.

Bacon, Roy, *Triumph Touring Twins: 1938–1966, Motorcycle Monograph No. 12* (Niton Publishing, ISBN 0-9514-204-6-1). This is one of Bacon's short but informative works, this time looking at the Speed Twin, Thunderbird and 3T. Also covers the Unit Construction 3TA and 5TA.

Bacon, Roy, *Triumph Tiger 100 & 110: 1939–1961, Motorcycle Monograph No. 5* (Niton Publishing, ISBN 0-9514-204-6-1). Covers the sporting Pre-units with lots of original factory images.

Bacon, Roy, *Triumph Twins and Triples* (Osprey Publishing, ISBN 0-85045-403-4). With its extensive listings of frame and engine numbers, specifications, and descriptions of all the Triumph twins, this is an invaluable work for any Triumph enthusiast.

Brooke, Lindsay and Gaylin, David, *Triumph Motorcycles in America* (Motor Books International Publishing, ISBN 0-87938-746-7). This book looks at the American side of the Triumph story, from its early days to the final demise of the Meriden Triumph in the 1980s, and the emergence of the new John Bloor-era Triumphs in the 1990s.

Clew, Jeff, *Turner's Triumphs — Edward Turner and his Triumph Motorcycles* (Veloce Publishing, ISBN 1-901295-87-7). A comprehensive history of the life of Edward Turner, well illustrated with lots of detail and a great read.

Davies, Ivor, *Triumph* (The Crowood Press, ISBN 1-86126-149-7). A fine historical record of Triumph, from its earliest beginnings through to the re-emergence of the name in the 1990s. It includes transcripts of many letters written by Turner throughout his time at Triumph, as well as many anecdotes and technical details of the bikes.

Davies, Ivor, *It's a Triumph, A Foulis Motorcycling Book* (Haynes Publishing, ISBN 0-85429-182-2). Written by a Triumph advertising manger, this is a good history of the company from its early days to the early 1960s. It has lots of insider anecdotes and also includes the text of Turner's 1960 report on the Japanese motor cycle industry.

Davies, Ivor, *It's Easy on a Triumph, A Foulis Motorcycling Book* (Haynes Publishing, ISBN 0-85429-786-3). A copiously illustrated gallop through the history of Triumph by factory man Ivor Davies, sprinkled with anecdotes and stories.

Gaylin, David, *Triumph Motorcycle Restoration Guide, Bonneville and TR6 1956-1983* (Motor Books International Publishing, ISBN 0-7603-0183-2). This book tracks the year-on-year specifications of the T120 and TR6 between 1956 and 1983, concentrating on the US models. It is liberally illustrated with diagrams and photographs of original and restored bikes, and is an excellent reference work and good read.

Hancox, Hughie, *Tales of Triumph and the Meriden Factory* (Veloce Publishing PLC, ISBN 1 901295 67 2). Hughie Hancox has an impeccable Triumph pedigree, starting with the company in 1954 and working for 'The Triumph' through to 1974, with a break for his national service, much of which was spent riding Triumphs in the White Helmets. This well-written and very readable book tells of his experiences at Triumph. After leaving Meriden, he ran a successful business restoring and servicing Meriden Triumphs.

Hopwood, Bert, *Whatever Happened to the British Motorcycle Industry?* (Haynes Publishing, ISBN 1-85960-427-7). This is the definitive history of the downfall of the British motorcycle industry, following the career of Bert Hopwood, who worked for most of the influential manufacturers from before World War Two to the industry's demise in the early 1970s.

Louis, Harry and Currie, Bob, *The Story of Triumph Motorcycles* (Patrick Stephens Ltd, ISBN 0-85059-671-8). This is a good history of the Triumph company from its origins in 1884 to 1983 and the final stillborn Meriden twins.

Nelson, John R., *Bonnie* (Haynes Publishing, ISBN 1-85429-957-2). With detailed year-on-year specifications this is an excellent and comprehensive description of the development of the T120 Bonneville, written by ex-Triumph Service Manager John Nelson.

Nelson, John R., *Triumph Tiger 100 and Daytona* (Haynes Publishing, ISBN 1-85960-428-5). This book provides an excellent and comprehensive description of the year-on-year specification and development of the Tiger 100 models, both Pre-unit and Unit.

Orchard, Chris and Maddon, Steve, *British Forces Motor Cycles, 1925–45* (Sutton Publishing, ISBN 0-7509-4451-X). This is a comprehensive guide to the motor cycles used by the British military up to and including World War Two. It includes a comprehensive section on Triumph and the 3TW.

Shilton, Neale, *A Million Miles Ago* (Haynes Publishing, ISBN 0 85429 313 2). After wartime service, Neale Shilton joined Triumph in 1946 as an area representative. He remained in the company until 1968 and in that time witnessed many important events. His book gives a graphic insight into working at 'The Triumph' and for Turner, in the 1940s, '50s and '60s.

Wilson, Steve, *Triumph T120/T140 Bonneville* (Haynes, ISBN 1-85960-679-2). This book covers the whole life of the T120 Bonneville, both Pre-unit and Unit Construction and covers the later 750cc variants as well. It gives a good, comprehensive description of the Pre-unit Bonnie.

Wilson, Steve, *British Motor Cycles Since 1950 Volume 5, Triumph Part One: The Company* (Patrick Stephens Ltd, ISBN 1-85260-021-7) and Wilson, Steve, British Motor Cycles Since 1950 Volume 6, Triumph The Bikes; Velocette and Vincent-HRD (Patrick Stephens Ltd, ISBN 1-85260-392-5). Produced by a motorcycling author and journalist with impeccable credentials, this pair of books covers both the Triumph company and the bikes (250cc and over) it produced from 1950. It is very well written and gives a really good account of the bikes and the politics behind them.

Woolridge, Harry, *The Triumph Speed Twin and Thunderbird Bible* (Veloce Publishing Ltd, ISBN 1-904788-26-2). Written by an ex-Meriden man, this book gives year-on-year specifications for the 5T and 6T models, from the Speed Twin's introduction in the 1938 model year through to the eventual demise of the 650cc Thunderbird in 1966. Well written and illustrated, with lots of detail, and lavishly illustrated with original factory pictures and diagrams.

Woolridge, Harry, *The Triumph Trophy Bible* (Veloce Publishing Ltd, ISBN 1-903706-12-2). This book gives year-on-year specifications of the TR5 and TR6 Trophy models, both Pre-unit and Unit Construction, and the Unit Construction TR6 and TR7 Tiger models. Well written and illustrated and a fine source of detailed information.

Museums and Collections

The UK has a rich cultural heritage, which includes a large number of museums with motorcycling exhibits. The following museums have Pre-unit Triumphs on display. It is not an exhaustive list, rather it includes museums that the author is aware of and has visited.

The Brooklands Museum concentrates on pre-war bikes and cars with a Brooklands connection, along with Hawker, Vickers and BAC aircraft. The main Triumph exhibit is the Titch Allen-built replica of Ivan Wicksteed and Marius Winslow's supercharged Speed Twin.

Brooklands Museum Trust Ltd, Brooklands Road, Weybridge, Surrey KT13 0QN

www.brooklandsmuseum.com

The London Motorcycle Museum was founded by Triumph dealer Bill Crosby and as well as housing his personal collection of Triumphs, has examples of most of the Pre-unit Triumph twins on display. The prototype swinging arm-framed TRW and the original 7ST 750cc side valve twin are a pair of notable exhibits, as are a 5TW prototype, a lightweight TRW prototype and a pre-war Tiger 80 single, showing Turner's styling skills.

The London Motorcycle Museum, Ravenor Farm, Oldfield Lane South, Greenford, Middlesex UB6 9LD

www.london-motorcycle-museum.org.

The National Motor Museum, at Beaulieu, Hampshire, while mainly a car-orientated collection, does have as significant number of bikes on display, including a number of Pre-unit Triumphs. Probably its most important Triumph is one of the original Montlhéry Circuit Thunderbirds (JAC 769), although the museum makes little fuss about it! In addition it has the last remaining military 3TW, a nicely sectioned 1948 Speed Twin and an impressive Café Racer, based around a duplex frame 650.

The National Motor Museum, Beaulieu, Brockenhurst, Hampshire, SO42 7ZN

www.nationalmotormuseum.org.uk

The National Motorcycle Museum at Birmingham has a huge range of British bikes on display, including a large range of Pre-unit Triumphs. These including examples of the girder forked pre-war Speed Twin and Tiger 100, and many post-war examples of Speed Twins, Tiger 100s, TR5 Trophies, Tiger 110s and T120 Bonnevilles. Among the Bonnevilles is a fine example of the first year's production model in Tangerine, complete with nacelle. The collection also boasts a single example of the 350cc 3T, a made up example of the 750cc 'Jumbo' 7ST side valve twin, using an original engine and standard 6T running gear, and the only surviving example of the 3TU. It also has a complete Triumph World War Two generator and an example of the 1930s' Val Page-designed 6-1 650cc twin.

The National Motorcycle Museum, Coventry Road, Bickenhill, Solihull, West Midlands, B92 0EJ

www.nationalmotorcyclemuseum.co.uk

The Sammy Miller Museum, in the New Forest at New Milton, Hampshire, has a wide range of bikes including a lovely 1952 TR5 Trophy, a 1958 Tiger 100 and an original Triumph GP racer (signed by Ernie Lyons). In addition, the museum also has the prototype Douglas DV60 and the Norton side valve twins that competed with the TRW for the Ministry of Supply Standard Military Motorcycle contract and a privately completed dohc eight-valve conversion of a 6T engine.

Sammy Miller Museum, Bashley Cross Roads, New Milton, Hampshire, BH25 5SZ.

www.sammymiller.co.uk

INDEX